WHATEVER IT TAKES

Men's Edition

James J. Holden
with
Adessa Holden

Whatever It Takes: Living A Life Worthy Of Your Calling

Copyright © 2019 Mantour Ministries

All rights reserved. No portion of this book may be reproduced, stored in a retrieval system, or transmitted in any form or by any means—electronic, mechanical, photocopy, recording, scanning, or other—except for brief quotations in reviews or articles, without the prior written permission of the author.
Published by 4One Ministries, Inc. Visit www.mantourministries.com for more information on bulk discounts and special promotions, or e-mail your questions to info@4oneministries.org.

All Scripture quotations, unless otherwise indicated, are taken from the Holy Bible, New International Version®, NIV®. Copyright ©1973, 1978, 1984, 2011 by Biblica, Inc.™ Used by permission of Zondervan. All rights reserved worldwide. www.zondervan.com The "NIV" and "New International Version" are trademarks registered in the United States Patent and Trademark Office by Biblica, Inc.™

Scripture quotations marked KJV are taken from the King James Version®. King James Version. Dallas, TX: Brown Books Publishing, 2004. Used by permission. All rights reserved.

Scripture quotations marked (NLT) are taken from the Holy Bible, New Living Translation, copyright © 1996, 2004, 2007 by Tyndale House Foundation. Used by permission of Tyndale House Publishers, Inc., Carol Stream, Illinois 60188. All Scripture taken from the New Century Version®. Copyright © 2005 by Thomas Nelson. Used by permission. All rights reserved.

Scripture quotations from THE MESSAGE. Copyright © by Eugene H. Peterson 1993, 1994, 1995, 1996, 2000, 2001, 2002. Used by permission of NavPress. All rights reserved. Represented by Tyndale House Publishers, Inc.

Design: James J. Holden

The author wishes to recognize Adessa Holden for her contribution to the text as an integral part of 4One Ministries, Adessa has participated in numerous editorial sessions and has willing shared her words during the creation of this work to advance God's Kingdom.

Subject Headings:
1. Christian life 2. Men's Ministry 3. Spiritual Growth

ISBN 978-1-7338505-2-0
ISBN 978-1-7338505-3-7 (ebook)
Printed in the United States of America

WHAT PEOPLE ARE SAYING ABOUT WHATEVER IT TAKES: LIVING A LIFE WORTHY OF YOUR CALLING:

"Through personal sacrifice, endurance through pain, and a commitment to a strong work ethic, Jamie and Adessa are leaders who practice what they preach. They are committed to do **Whatever it Takes** and will challenge you and your group to follow the call of God in your life, walk in personal holiness, and be filled with the Holy Spirit."

– **Tom Rees,** *PennDel Ministry Network Men's Ministry Director*

"Jesus calls us to '*deny ourselves, take up our cross and follow Him*' but too many people want five easy steps to significance; not the cross. In **Whatever It Takes** Jamie gives important practical, biblical principles for fulfilling God's call to follow Jesus and effectively use your gifts and service to build up the Kingdom of God.

Jamie actually mentors you from what he has learned from others, his own experience, and doing ministry. I was pleased to find that the principles he has chosen to include are ones I modeled and trained our Pastoral and ministry teams to incorporate in their lives and ministry.

There is no short cut to laying a foundation of mature character and spiritual growth upon which all our ministry is built. **Whatever It Takes** will definitely inspire and encourage you to passionately pursue God's call for your life and live a life worthy of His calling."

-**Pastor Roland and Angela Coon,** *Presbyter, Delmarva Section of the PennDel Ministry Network, 4One Ministries Board of Directors*

"We're thankful for ministers who are bold enough to bring the full truth of the word of God. Jamie and Adessa Holden deliver that truth in a strong manner while handling each topic with gentleness and wisdom."

-**Pastor Joey and Lori Cullen,** *Philadelphia Master's Commission Directors, 4One Ministries Board of Directors*

"What a privilege to endorse and recommend ***Whatever it Takes***, written by Jamie and Adessa Holden.

Whether you are called by God to minister across the street from where you live, or across the ocean in a foreign land, this book is definitely a powerful tool to assist you in seeing what that calling can look like as you obey the *voice recognition* of the precious Holy Spirit and *embrace the call* that God has placed upon your life.

As you read and study each portion of this book, your life will be both enriched and challenged as you fulfill the perfect will of God for your life.

Jamie and Adessa have a beautiful gift of conveying the very heart of God as they share personal experiences in their life, inspirational testimonies from the places God has called them, and numerous Scripture references to bring everything back to God and His Word.

Don't wait another minute to dive into ***Whatever it Takes***! You'll absolutely be glad you did!"

-**Pastor John and Susan Lanza,** *Glad Tidings Assembly of God*

"Jamie and Adessa's passion for people is evident in the pages of ***Whatever It Takes*** as they urge the reader to abandon the world, every part of it, and walk in the calling God has for them.

Using solid, Biblical teaching, they share scriptures and real-life stories to teach truth in a way that's easily understandable.

Each chapter ends with questions that are appropriate for individual or group study.

It isn't often that a book comes along to challenge the reader using such realistic examples of how to put faith into action.

-**Pastor Wayne and Suzanne Schaffer,** *New Life Worship Center*

DEDICATION

We would like to dedicate this book, **Whatever It Takes**, to a couple that constantly inspires us to live a life worthy of our calling, to hold fast to our convictions, and to boldly share Biblical truth with others. The truth is that whenever we find ourselves asking, *"Are we being too old-fashioned? Are Christians still called to reach for a higher standard and live a life worthy of our calling?"* this couple's example and dedication to Jesus and ministry compel us to not only maintain our commitment, but to reach even further.

For your friendship, your dedication to serving Jesus and people, and the standard and the example you set for us, we are dedicating this book to **Pastor Phil and Carol Menditto**. We are honored to have you in our lives and deeply touched that you call us friends. Thank you for always doing **Whatever It Takes**.

TABLE OF CONTENTS

1	Whatever It Takes	9
2	Embracing The Call	17
3	So You Think You Have A Choice?	25
4	Voice Recognition	35
5	Connecting To Your Power Source	43
6	Taking The Leap	59
7	The Price Is Right	69
8	You Don't Know What You Don't Know	83
9	Higher Standards	93
10	Honesty Really Is The Best Policy	111
11	Love Really Is A Verb	121
12	Defeat Is NOT An Option	137
	Workbook	149
	Fill In Answers	183
	Bibliography	185

Chapter One

Whatever It Takes

"Come, follow me," Jesus said, "and I will send you out to fish for people." (Matthew 4:19, NIV)

The year was 1994, and I was driving to the small Christian school I attended about 25 minutes away from home. The whole trip was back country roads, and I'd have my windows open and the latest in Christian music blaring as high as it could go. Back in the day before iTunes or Spotify, almost every young teen joined what was called the Columbia House Tape Club where you got twelve cassettes for a penny each…what a deal! One of my twelve cassettes was the greatest hits of Steven Curtis Chapman, and I played this cassette regularly on my treks to school.

One of Steven Curtis Chapman's greatest hits was the song *"For the Sake of the Call"*. I loved singing along at the top of my lungs to this song that talked about the *"crazy fishermen"* who left everything to follow Jesus simply because He called them. Still, it would be years later that the Holy Spirit caused the lyrics from that song to burn inside of my heart as He asked me, *"Will you, like Peter, follow Jesus with reckless abandon? Will you follow God's plan for your life, even if it is different than your plan for your life?"*

Over the years of my life, I have been faced with this question over and over again as God repeatedly asked me to take new leaps of faith, to follow Him blindly wherever He leads, to go boldly into new areas of life and ministry, to give EVERYTHING up for Him, and to do whatever it takes to follow His calling on my life. Over and over, I have made the reckless decision to follow Jesus. Even though I didn't always know where that would take me, I knew that I loved Jesus and wanted His will for my life.

These decisions all began with the day I once and for all told God that, no matter what He called me to do, where He called me to go, and whatever He decided He wanted me to be, I was all in. I'd do whatever it takes to walk in His calling. It was the day I decided to give my whole life to Jesus with absolute abandon.

I guess it could be compared to the day that a couple gets engaged. It's the big moment. At some point, the girl gets the guy to have *"the talk"* and he commits to a relationship with her. Then a little later, he goes all in. He saves every cent he has so he can go and pick out a ring. He works up the courage to ask her dad permission to propose, and he works up even more courage to ask her the big question. They both agree that *"yes"* they will spend the rest of their lives together. It's a day they will never forget—-a day they will recount to future generations—-the moment they will recall when days are difficult.

And yet, just like an engagement, it is only the beginning of the relationship. It's step one. The actual making of a happy marriage isn't as magical as fairy tales and Hallmark Christmas movies would like to make us think. (Yes, I watch Hallmark Christmas movies, and no, you cannot have my man-card back.) A couple coming together, declaring their love and deciding to get married doesn't always guarantee a happily ever after. It is only the beginning. As any married person will tell you, actually living happily together forever takes a lot of work, a commitment to endure the difficult times, and a willingness to accept the responsibilities that come with a loving, committed relationship.

Over the past twenty years of walking with God, I have learned that the same principles apply to living out a person's God-given calling. Because while, yes, hearing God's voice call you to salvation or leading you into His direction for your life is exhilarating and exciting, while it is momentous and life-changing, it, too, is only the beginning. It's the first step in a lifelong journey that will require work, obedience, sacrifice, commitment, and a willingness to accept the responsibilities that come with living a life worthy of your calling.

Sadly, this truth is a stumbling block for many followers of Jesus. They don't want to do whatever it takes to answer God's call.

Yes, they love the idea of having a calling. They are ecstatic about the idea that the God of the Universe would have a plan and a purpose for their lives—-a role for them in His kingdom—-a job that only they can accomplish. When they first hear the Holy Spirit's voice during a conference or at an altar or during a time of prayer, they are thrilled. They are overwhelmed with joy. They cannot wait to begin walking in God's plan for their lives! It's going to be amazing!

Then reality begins to set in. The true test of their commitment is seen when following God's will for their lives begins to require sacrifice, obedience, and commitment. When the Holy Spirit begins asking them to live a life worthy of their calling, too many would-be followers of Jesus begin looking for an escape clause. Eventually settling into a life of wishy-washy compromise, they either choose to abdicate the call of God on their lives or live beneath their calling, never fully experiencing all that God has for them or accomplishing all that He wants for His kingdom.

It's like the parable of the soils in Matthew 13:

Study this story of the farmer planting seed.

> *"The seed cast in the gravel—this is the person who hears and instantly responds with enthusiasm. But there is no soil of character, and so when the emotions wear off and some difficulty arrives, there is nothing to show for it.*
>
> *The seed cast in the weeds is the person who hears the kingdom news, but weeds of worry and illusions about getting more and wanting everything under the sun strangle what was heard, and nothing comes of it.*
>
> *The seed cast on good earth is the person who hears and takes in the News, and then produces a harvest beyond his wildest dreams." (Matthew 13:18, 20-23, The Message)*

This is the choice that each of us needs to make regarding God's call on our lives: After we initially respond with enthusiasm, will we continue our passionate pursuit by actually living out our calling?

> **"Whatever it takes, yes, Lord Jesus, I will follow You in every area of my life."**

Looking at my own life, I can testify that this is a choice that each of us will have to make more than once throughout our journey with Jesus. It's a decision we have to make almost daily as we choose whether or not we will live a life worthy of our calling.

Will we walk in obedience each day? Will we make the necessary sacrifices? Will we follow God no matter where He leads or what responsibilities He asks us to accept? It's not as dramatic as an altar experience. Instead, it's a quiet resolve that daily says, *"Whatever it takes, yes, Lord Jesus, I will follow You in every area of my life."*

This resolve is the core of living a life worthy of your calling.

It's moving beyond the moment when God pops the question and resolving in your heart that, whatever it takes, you will follow Jesus.

It's this aspect of our calling that we are going to explore in this book. We'll discuss some of the choices each of us will need to make to live out our God-given calling in every aspect of our lives. Then we'll get personal and practical as each chapter will also contain what I like to call *"radical challenges"*—-simple, practical steps that you and I can take to implement the principles we will talk about in our everyday lives.

I hope that as we take this journey together, you will be encouraged and inspired to passionately pursue God's call for your life and live a life worthy of your calling.

Because here is one final truth that I have learned on my journey to walking with God—-it's the promise that is found at the end of the parable of the soils.

> *The seed cast on good earth is the person who hears and takes in the News, and then produces a harvest beyond his wildest dreams. (Matthew 13:23, The Message)*

Here's an important truth: Choosing to follow Jesus and walk in your calling will require work and sacrifice, obedience and commitment. However, it will also reap rewards that are beyond anything you can imagine.

Ephesians 3:20-21 says:

> *God can do anything, you know—far more than you could*

> *ever imagine or guess or request in your wildest dreams! He does it not by pushing us around but by working within us, his Spirit deeply and gently within us. (The Message)*

This is a truly amazing aspect! The God of the Universe has a plan for your life. From the beginning of time, He's had a plan to advance His kingdom, and that plan includes a role for YOU. Today, He is calling your name and saying, *"Do you want to play the part I have for you?"*

Just like the original disciples who went from being fishermen from the small town of Galilee to being world changers, God has a plan for your life that goes WAY above and beyond anything you can imagine. He has a destiny He wants you to fulfill. A life that is so much richer and more meaningful than you could even dream.

Now the choice lies with you.

Do you want to walk in God's call for your life?

Do you want to find God's perfect will for your life, your destiny, the reason you were created, and the job God has for you?

As you discover your calling, are you willing to do whatever it takes to walk in your calling?

Are you willing to abandon it all for the sake of the call?

If you are ready to say, *"Yes!"* then let's get started with the rest of the book and begin doing whatever it takes to live a life worthy of our calling.

Group Study Questions:

1. How is accepting God's call similar to a marriage engagement?

2. What has been hindering you from walking confidently into God's calling?

3. This chapter stated, *"Choosing to follow Jesus and walk in your calling will require work and sacrifice, obedience and commitment."* What does this mean to you?

4. As you discover your calling, are you willing to do whatever it takes to walk in your calling?

5. After reading this chapter, what is one thing you will put into practice or one thing you will change in your life?

6. How can we as a group help you do this?

Radical Challenge:

We must all remember our memorial stones—the moments when we hear God's call either to salvation or when He reveals a portion of His will for our lives.

This chapter's radical challenge is to take some time and remember one of these experiences. Record the incident on paper or a computer. Place it somewhere that you will always remember your commitment to do whatever it takes to follow God's will for your life.

Chapter Two
Embracing The Call

You are a chosen people. You are royal priests, a holy nation, God's very own possession. As a result, you can show others the goodness of God, for he called you out of the darkness into his wonderful light.
(1 Peter 2:9, NLT)

It was his big moment—the interview to see whether or not my friend would get the job of a lifetime. During the question and answer period, someone asked, *"Why do you want this job?"*

Pausing for a moment to make sure he answered properly, he said, *"It isn't so much about wanting the job, but rather that I feel that God has called me to serve in this position at this time."*

It was a surprising answer, and yet it perfectly sums up the attitude that every believer should have regarding how they live out their days on earth. It recognizes the truth that from the day we give our hearts to God and accept God's call to follow Him, our lives no longer belong to us. As Paul says in 2 Corinthians 5:15:

> ***He died for everyone so that those who receive his new life will no longer live for themselves.***
>
> ***Instead, they will live for Christ, who died and was raised for them. (NLT)***

This is a very important concept for every believer. Before you came to God, you could pretty much live your life as you pleased under the laws of free will. However, when you came to God, you surrendered your life to Him.

It's much like someone who joins the armed services. I love our military men, and I am so grateful to every man and woman who enlists to defend this great country of ours. These mighty warriors voluntarily give up their personal rights to direct their own life to join the armed services community. It's their choice to join the armed services, but after that, the armed services make most of the choices for them.

They tell them where they want them to go.

They decide where a soldier lives.

They choose a soldier's job and determine their rank.

Members of the armed services adopt their branch's code of conduct. They follow their rules and regulations. When they disobey, they accept the discipline.

A soldier doesn't get to decide whether or not they deploy or when they return home. They are sent on a mission and they are expected to obey.

Because they believe in the cause and want to serve their country, they submit to this lifestyle.

It's the same way when you surrender your life to God. You agree to live by His standards, follow His rules, and fulfill the role that He has for you in life. You are no longer the master of your own ship, but you are now committed to following the leading of the Holy Spirit in your life. Along with all of the benefits that come with the privilege of being a part of God's family, there is also the responsibility of fulfilling the unique role He designed for you to play in His kingdom. This is your ultimate purpose in life.

As we read throughout Scripture, we see that we were not put on this earth to simply exist. We aren't just a mass of cells with no design. Instead, we read in Scripture that before we were even born, God had a plan and a purpose for our lives.

> *You made all the delicate, inner parts of my body and knit me together in my mother's womb.*
>
> *Thank you for making me so wonderfully complex! Your workmanship is marvelous—how well I know it.*
>
> *You watched me as I was being formed in utter seclusion as I was woven together in the dark of the womb.*
>
> *You saw me before I was born. Every day of my life was recorded in your book.*
>
> *Every moment was laid out before a single day had passed. (Psalm 139:13-16, NLT)*

We see an example of this in God's call to Jeremiah:

> *I knew you before I formed you in your mother's womb. Before you were born I set you apart and appointed you as my prophet to the nations. (Jeremiah 1:5, NLT)*

And yet, this principle doesn't just apply to the prophet Jeremiah. God has an equally important purpose for each of us who choose to follow Him.

Here's a radical challenge: We were not born so that we could simply earn enough money to survive, live out our days in monotony, or experience as much pleasure as possible. Instead, God has a unique purpose just for you. He has a place that He wants you to fill.

His plan for your life doesn't just involve you, but instead, it involves the lives of every person that He wants you to reach and influence for the kingdom of God. Extending the circle even further, God's plan involves the people their lives will reach, and on and on it goes. The truth is that God's plan for your individual life is so much bigger than you can ever imagine or may even comprehend in your lifetime. It is part of His eternal plan to bring as many people as possible into a personal relationship with Him so that they can spend eternity with Him.

> **God's plan for your life doesn't just involve you, but instead, it involves the lives of every person that He wants you to reach and influence for the kingdom of God.**

In the grand scheme of things, God's plan is magnificent, unimaginable, eternal, and unfathomable. Yet, the truly amazing part is that in this humongous, incredible plan there is a part for you and me to play.

What an honor! What a privilege! And yet, as Uncle Ben told Spiderman *"With great privilege comes great responsibility."*[1]

It's almost overwhelming to think about, and yet we don't need to be overwhelmed because understanding the big picture is not up to us. Instead, our responsibility is to seek God's will for our own personal lives and then choose to serve where He puts us.

"But isn't this just for pastors and missionaries? Do you really believe that God has a plan for the life of every believer?"

Absolutely!

1 Peter 2:9 says:

> ***But you are not like that, for you are a chosen people. You are royal priests, a holy nation, God's very own possession.***
>
> ***As a result, you can show others the goodness of God, for he called you out of the darkness into his wonderful light. (NLT)***

Yes, it is true. In the Old Testament, only Levites were called to serve God as priests. However, this verse teaches us that under the New Testament covenant we are all chosen. We are all a royal priesthood. All believers have a calling to show God's goodness and be a witness in the world around them.

Whether God calls you to be His representative in a church, a school, a hospital, a grocery store, a factory, a bank, the military, a car dealership, or anywhere else, He has called you to that place so you can be an influence for the kingdom of God. More importantly, He needs you there to reach the people in that community for Him.

> **We need to be aware that our lives are not just our own—we belong to God.**

Whatever your place in life or your vocation, it is your calling to be a representative of God.

That's why it is so important that we understand this principle of calling. We need to be aware that our lives are not just our own—we belong to God.

As my friend said in his job interview, *"It's not about what I want. It's about seeking God's will for my life and doing whatever it takes to serve where He calls."*

As we understand this concept, we need to choose how we will respond. Will we, like the twelve disciples choose to follow God or will we turn away and say, *"No thanks. I'd rather not?"*

Because here is the sad truth: Many people choose to abdicate God's call on their lives.

They want what they want, the way they want it, and they will not submit to God's plan.

This is such a sad choice because while they are afraid of what they will miss if they follow God's call on their life, they aren't even considering all they are missing by abdicating God's call on their life.

Purpose. Destiny. Watching God take the little that you have to offer Him and use it in ways beyond anything you could dream or imagine.

The opportunity to make an eternal difference in the world.

The chance to partner with God to advance His kingdom and have the hours of your life reap eternal rewards.

What could be better than this?

It's all waiting for you as you answer God's call for your life.

And yet, the choice remains with you. God has a call—are you ready to answer it?

Group Study Questions:

1. What do you believe is your calling in life?

2. What does *"With great privilege comes great responsibility"* mean to you?

3. How does submitting to your God-given calling resemble joining the armed services?

4. How does this analogy change the way you think about your calling?

5. How does it affect other people when you do not walk in your calling?

6. Are you willing to embrace God's calling?

7. After reading this chapter, what is one thing you will put into practice or one thing you will change in your life?

8. How can we as a group help you do this?

Radical Challenge:

Do you realize that YOU were not born to simply earn enough money to survive, live out your days in monotony, or experience as much pleasure as possible?

Do you recognize that God has a unique purpose just for you—that purpose includes influencing people in your sphere of influence for the kingdom of God?

As a practical step, grab a sheet of paper and make a list of the people in your life—including family, friends, co-workers, people in your community. Ask God, *"How do You want me to influence them for You?"*

Chapter Three

So You Think You Have A Choice?

Turning his head, Peter noticed the disciple Jesus loved following right behind. When Peter noticed him, he asked Jesus, "Master, what's going to happen to him?"
Jesus said, "If I want him to live until I come again, what's that to you? You—follow me."
(John 21:20-22, The Message)

Beyond a doubt, this has always been one of my favorite stories in the Bible.

Peter and Jesus are walking together on the beach after one of the most momentous occasions of Peter's life. They'd just finished their big talk. A resurrected Jesus offered Peter forgiveness, restoration, and a renewal of his calling after Peter's betrayal and denial. It was the moment when Jesus said, *"Even though you failed, I know your heart, and you're still My guy. I still want you on My team. I still have a plan and a purpose for your life."* Then He reaffirmed Peter's calling with the words, *"Follow Me".*

It was a life-changing conversation that Peter would remember forever. If Hollywood were writing the scene, it would have ended there with ***"Follow Me"*** in a logo and a monstrous anthem as credits rolled, maybe followed by a post-credit scene of the disciples and Jesus cleaning fish and cracking jokes around a fire. But the Bible is real life and Peter was a very real person as evidenced by what he said next.

> ***Turning his head, Peter noticed the disciple Jesus loved following right behind. When Peter noticed him, he asked Jesus, "Master, what's going to happen to him?"***
> ***(John 21-20-21, The Message)***

This is why I love Peter!!! He makes the same mistakes as so many of us! Because if we are all honest, we have to admit, we've asked this question ourselves many times. Too often when God wants to lead us into our unique calling, we ask, *"But what about them?"*

Of course, it sounds different when we ask it. It sounds more like:

"Can I have a calling like theirs?" or *"Why don't they have to walk the same road You're asking me to travel?"*

I'd imagine our questions are met with the same response that Jesus gave to Peter. I can almost see Jesus laughing as He puts His arm on Peter's shoulder and saying, *"Dude, what about them? What I do in their lives is between Me and them. Don't worry about it, you follow Me."* (My personal paraphrase of John 21:22.)

I remember earlier in my ministry, I really had to put this principle into practice. When God called me to start ministering to men and then to start Mantour Ministries, I really struggled with feelings of inferiority. Who was I to minister to men? I in no way fit into the stereotypical model of a men's minister…a man who had a great marriage, was a great father, was athletic, and had all the answers men needed. That was not me.

How could I, as a single man who has never been married, has never even changed a diaper and has no kids of my own, was disabled, and had no connections or path to ministry, ever minister to men? We had no names to drop or family connections…as one friend said to me recently, *"You guys just came out of nowhere!"* Did God really want Adessa and I to be the *"Donny and Marie"* of ministry teams and minister together as brother and sister? Could I be effective with all these against-the-norm-areas of my life?

As I continued mulling the issue in my mind and in prayer, one word kept coming back into my mind. The word was *"calling."*

All I needed to follow God was to stop looking at what I thought I needed to be and instead start looking at where God was leading me and what He was calling me to do. It didn't matter if I was single. It didn't matter if I never had kids. It didn't matter that I couldn't throw a football, or play on a softball team. All that mattered was knowing that God called me. I had to choose to get my eyes off of everyone and everything else and follow His call.

> **"Calling" puts the responsibility on God to decide who is "allowed" to do what in His kingdom.**

Why is *"calling"* so important?

Because *"calling"* puts the responsibility on God to decide who is *"allowed"* to do what in His kingdom. It frees us from this burden and allows us to be free to follow God's call on our lives.

From this perspective, I have come to believe that anyone can do anything God has called them to do, whether man or woman, single or married, young or old.

Of course, this change in perspective carries with it the enormous responsibility of seeking God's will for our lives rather than simply making choices on our own.

This is a very important distinction because we live in a society that tells us that we have unlimited choices in our lives. We can have any life we choose and have everything we want.

Yet, as a Christian, I don't see where this concept of choice is Biblical. As we said in the last chapter, as Christians we all have a calling—a purpose God wants us to fulfill. Rather than being able to choose what we want to do, it is our personal responsibility to spend time earnestly and actively seeking God's will for our lives.

We can see proof of this if we go back just a few verses in John 20 and take a look at a previous part of the conversation between Jesus and Peter.

> *Then he said it a third time: "Simon, son of John, do you love me?"*
>
> *Peter was upset that he asked for the third time, "Do you love me?" so he answered, "Master, you know everything there is to know. You've got to know that I love you."*
>
> *Jesus said, "Feed my sheep. I'm telling you the very truth now:*
>
> *When you were young you dressed yourself and went wherever you wished, but when you get old you'll have to stretch out your hands while someone else dresses you and takes you where you don't want to go."*

> *He said this to hint at the kind of death by which Peter would glorify God.*
>
> *And then he commanded, "Follow me."*
>
> *(John 20:17-19, The Message)*

In these verses, we see Jesus teaching Peter that before He became a follower of Christ, Peter could choose what he wanted to do with his life. However, now things have changed. Having answered God's call, Peter's life now belonged to God. From this point forward, God would be directing his life and it would be Peter's responsibility to obey.

This principle doesn't just apply to Peter. Instead, it applies to all of us who call ourselves followers of Christ. As such, our lives no longer belong to us, they belong to God. He purchased them with His blood at Calvary.

As 2 Corinthians 5:15 says, **"He died for everyone so that those who receive this new life will no longer live for themselves. Instead, they will live for Christ, who died and was raised for them." (NLT)**

That's why it is so important that as followers of Christ, we willingly accept the responsibility to seek God's will for our lives. Practically, this means that we don't just make decisions based on what society says is normal, what everyone else is doing, or even on what we want to do with our lives. Instead, every choice that we make in our lives needs to be proceeded with prayer and a passionate pursuit that asks **"Heavenly Father, what do You want to do with my life? Which road do You want me to take so that I will continue to walk in your unique calling for my life?"**

This applies to all of the roles that we play in life. We should be seeking God's will in all areas of our lives. It shouldn't just be a one time question, but rather a lifestyle of praying about every decision and making every choice through the lens of *"What is God's will for my life in this situation?"*

Rather than making choices on our own, I believe, as Christians, we should be asking God:

Who do you want me dating and eventually marrying?

How many kids should we have?

What job do you want me to take?

Do you want me to take this promotion or stay where I am? Is the money worth the sacrifice in other areas?

> **The phrase "unique calling" is very important. God doesn't call us all to do the same thing.**

Where should I live?

What car should I drive?

Where should I volunteer?

What church do You want me to attend?

This is just a brief list of the areas where we should be seeking God's will and calling on our lives rather than simply making our own choices. I truly believe that as we pray and spend time seeking God's will, then God will be faithful to show us which choice each one of us needs to make to follow the unique calling that He has for our lives.

Again, the phrase *"unique calling"* is very important. God doesn't call us all to do the same thing. While He may call one guy to be a policeman, He may call another to teach in a public school. One man may be called to be a lawyer, while another is called to be an accountant, and another is called to be a mechanic. The truth is that no calling is any more or less valuable than another. They are all equal because they all come from God and they all fulfill God's unique plan for the life of a specific individual.

As it says in 1 Corinthians 12:12-18:

> *You can easily enough see how this kind of thing works by looking no further than your own body.*
>
> *Your body has many parts—limbs, organs, cells—but no matter how many parts you can name, you're still one body. It's exactly the same with Christ.*
>
> *By means of his one Spirit, we all said good-bye to our partial and piecemeal lives. We each used to independently call our own shots, but then we entered into a large and integrated life in which he has the final say in everything. (This is what we proclaimed in word and action when we were baptized.)*
>
> *Each of us is now a part of his resurrection body, refreshed and sustained at one fountain—his Spirit—where we all come to drink. The old labels we once used to identify ourselves—labels like Jew or Greek, slave or free—are no longer useful. We need something larger, more comprehensive.*
>
> *I want you to think about how all this makes you more significant, not less.*
>
> *A body isn't just a single part blown up into something huge. It's all the different-but-similar parts arranged and functioning together.*
>
> *If Foot said, "I'm not elegant like Hand, embellished with rings; I guess I don't belong to this body," would that make it so?*
>
> *If Ear said, "I'm not beautiful like Eye, limpid and expressive; I don't deserve a place on the head," would you want to remove it from the body?*

> *If the body was all eye, how could it hear? If all ear, how could it smell?*
>
> *As it is, we see that God has carefully placed each part of the body right where he wanted it. (The Message)*

That's where Jesus' conversation with Peter becomes so ridiculously practical in our lives. We are not called to sit in judgment or criticism over what God has called another person to do. Really, it is none of our business. Instead, each of us needs to take on the personal responsibility to make sure that we are following Jesus.

Each of us needs to choose to seek God's will in each area of our lives and obey the unique calling He gives us.

When we have truly sought God's will and we can say with a clear conscience, *"I believe that this is what God has called me to do with my life,"* then I believe that we are free to do whatever He has called us to do without restriction.

Going hand in hand with that, we need to allow other people the same freedom to follow their own unique, God-given calling in life. Rather than criticizing them, being jealous of them, or trying to tear each other down, we need to be supporting each other, believing that God is using each of us to play our unique role in building God's kingdom.

So what can you do in God's kingdom?

Anything God calls you to do.

The question is, *"Are you passionately pursuing your calling?"*

Let's get specific and personal and ask:

When you need to make a decision or choose a life path, are you seeking God's will or making decisions on your own? This really is the first step in passionately pursuing your calling.

So You Think You Have A Choice?

Are you open to the Holy Spirit to lead you into God's unique call for your life? What if it's something you may not have planned or imagined? Are you willing to follow God into an unexpected area?

As I said earlier, this has been a challenge for me throughout my walk with God as His plans for my life have been bigger, bolder, and more adventurous than I would have imagined. Yet, I've learned that it is only as we find our place living out God's unique plan for our lives and fulfilling His kingdom purpose that we truly find satisfaction, peace, contentment, and fulfillment.

From this place, we don't have to ask, *"What about them?"* We'll be too busy following God's plan for our own lives.

Group Study Questions:

1. Why do you think we struggle with looking at other people's calling instead of focusing on what God has called us to do?

2. Why is it unbiblical to say that we, as God's children, can have any life we choose and have everything we want?

3. How do we discover our unique calling?

4. What practical steps can you take to encourage others to follow their unique calling?

5. Are you passionately pursuing your calling?

6. After reading this chapter, what is one thing you will put into practice or one thing you will change in your life?

7. How can we as a group help you do this?

Radical Challenge:

Make a list of the decisions you currently need to make in your life.

Commit to seeking God's will in prayer about each decision. As the Holy Spirit leads you in each area, take a moment and write down how God directed you in each choice. Then follow God's leading even if it is different than you originally planned.

Commit to making this a new practice in your life.

Chapter Four

Voice Recognition

My sheep listen to my voice; I know them, and they follow me.
(John 10:27, NIV)

Have you ever been in a room full of people talking when you recognize one voice among the crowd?

Perhaps it's the laugh of a significant other, the cry of a child, or the voice of a friend. Maybe you hear them call your name and you know immediately who is trying to get your attention. Even among all of the other noise and conversations in the room, like radar, you are tuned into this voice.

I'm sure we've all been there. I know I have. Many times I've been in a room full of people when I hear my sister yell, *"Jamie."* Because I'm so familiar with her voice (after all, I hear it every day,) I instantly know who is calling me. In fact, I'm so familiar with her voice that I can tell from her tone if she's telling a joke, if she's angry, if I forgot something, if she is not feeling well, if she needs me to help her with something, or she just wants me to join her conversation. It doesn't matter how many other people are in the room because her voice is so familiar to me, it always rises above the crowd. As soon as I hear it, she has my attention.

Whenever I read Jesus teaching about His sheep hearing His voice in John 10, this is the picture that comes into my mind. Because, I don't know about you, but I'm not as up on my sheep/shepherd metaphors as the people in the New Testament. Sheep aren't really my thing. Still, after a little research, I learned some interesting facts.

For instance, did you know that in New Testament times they would keep several flocks in the same sheep pen? Every morning, the shepherd called out his sheep to follow him to the spot where they would go and graze for the day.

How did the sheep know which shepherd to follow?

Each shepherd had a peculiar call with which he led his sheep. Even though sheep have a reputation for being notoriously dense, the one thing they clearly recognize is their shepherd's call. When they hear it, they follow.

> **As followers of God seeking to live a life worthy of our calling, we are to be as familiar with the voice of God as a sheep is to its shepherd's voice.**

Here's the part that really intrigued me: The sheep cannot be fooled. They are so in tune with their individual shepherd's voice that they refuse to follow a stranger because his voice was unfamiliar. In fact, if a stranger should use the shepherd's call and imitate his tone, the flock would instantly detect the difference and would scatter in panic.[1] Yet, when they hear their shepherd's voice—-they immediately obey. Talk about familiarity!!!

Of course, the lesson in this parable is that as followers of God seeking to live a life worthy of our calling, we are to be as familiar with the voice of God as a sheep is to its shepherd's voice. His voice is supposed to be so familiar to us that we recognize it and respond to it just like we recognize and respond to the voice of those who are closest to us.

In the last chapter, we talked about our personal responsibility to seek and follow God's unique call in our individual lives. Yet many people ask, *"How do I do that? How do I know what God wants me to do?"*

The answer is that we need to spend time with God asking for His guidance and listening for His response.

But how can we be sure it is God talking to us?

The answer is familiarity.

Just like we are familiar with the voices of those with whom we spend the most time, we need to be familiar with the voice of God. His voice needs to be so familiar to us that it rises above the voice of the crowds, of society, of the people around us, and even our thoughts. Like the sheep who know the voice of their shepherd, we need to be that familiar with the voice of the Holy Spirit.

And yet, this level of familiarity doesn't magically happen. Instead, it only happens as we choose to spend time with God so that we can become familiar with the sound of His voice and learn to recognize it. This is why a large part of our responsibility to do whatever it takes to live a life worthy of our calling is choosing to spend dedicated time alone with God every day.

Yes, I know, I hear it all the time…people are busy. Our lives are over-scheduled. There is just too much to do and not enough time to do it. Because life is so busy, many people believe the lie that they don't have time to spend dedicated time alone with God in prayer and Bible reading. However, the truth that I have learned over decades of walking with God is that this lie is one of the main reasons that too many Christians are living below their calling.

Because they aren't spending time with God, they aren't familiar with His voice.

This lack of familiarity keeps them from hearing God lead them in every area of our lives.

If you can't recognize God's voice, you can't obey it and walk in the calling that God has for your life.

One of the lies that the enemy is using to keep Christians from experiencing all that God has for them in life is that *"Prayerlessness and inconsistency in Bible reading is no big deal."* Yet, just like all of Satan's lies, believing this lie leads to nothing but heartache and destruction in our lives. If we want to walk in the fullness of the calling God has for us, then we need to denounce this lie and begin making proactive steps to daily spend time becoming familiar with the voice of God.

How do we do this? Well, here's where we need to accept some radical challenges:

#1 We need to recognize the importance of consistently spending time alone with God.

It's my experience that until we recognize the importance of something we don't prioritize it. How many times have you heard about someone who didn't implement diet and exercise into their lives until they had a health crisis? Then all of a sudden, something they didn't have time for becomes a priority.

> **Until we recognize the importance of something, we don't really prioritize it.**

Even more important than our physical health is our spiritual health. The first step in doing whatever it takes to become spiritually healthy is recognizing the incredible importance of being familiar with the voice of God. Then we will do whatever it takes to make it a priority in our lives.

#2 We need to schedule a time to be with God.

Over the years, I've learned that if you don't make time to pray, you won't find the time. That's why I believe it's important for each of us to take a hard look at our daily schedule and evaluate when a good time would be to establish a daily prayer time. Just like we look at our schedule and see when we can fit in a doctor's appointment, time at the gym, or lunch with a friend, we need to look at our schedule, see when we can make time, and then make a daily appointment to pray.

If you look at your schedule and can't find time to be alone with God for 15-30 minutes a day, then your schedule is too full. Something needs to go and be replaced by a time of prayer. Maybe it's sleep, maybe it's a hobby, but scheduling prayer needs to be a priority in the life of a believer.

#3 Tell the people in your life when you've scheduled a time to pray.

My sister has a friend who tells her family, *"This is the time that Mom sets aside to pray…unless someone is bleeding or dying, don't bother me. Trust me, you want Mom to pray…it makes your life better."*

Even though it sounds funny, this Mom has keyed into an important part of having a daily time with God.

I know a man who wanted to make spending time in the Word and with God a priority, so he kindly told his wife, *"I need you and the kids to let me alone for half an hour so I can do this."* Guys, you need to make the people in your life aware of your commitment so they can help you keep it. If they don't know what you're doing, they will think they can interrupt, but if they know this is the time you spend with God, they know to stay away.

#4 Find a comfortable, private place to pray.

I had heard a lot of people say they got on their face before God, meaning they lay face down on the floor. I am happy this works for them, but it just doesn't work for me. I always end up falling asleep! I have had to find a different place and posture to pray that works for me. Find a place to pray that is private (so you won't be distracted) yet comfortable. Make it *"your spot to be with your Father."* Again, let your family know that when you are there, they shouldn't interrupt. But don't make it too comfortable or you, like me, will doze off. Find a balance, and make it your place to pray.

#5 Keep your appointment

Sometimes we feel like we don't have anything to talk to God about that day. Other days, we feel like we are just too tired to pray. Don't let these excuses keep you from spending time with your Father. Instead, on those days, go to your spot and listen to praise music, speak in tongues, just sit and be quiet before God and listen to Him speak. Allow Him to refresh and refuel you so that you can continue walking in your calling.

#6 Start a Bible Reading Plan and Stick to It.

One of the best ways to become familiar with the voice of God is by reading the Bible daily. This is where we learn what God thinks, how He acts, how He feels, and what He expects from us.

There are many Bible reading plans from which you can choose. The important thing is that you pick one, start reading, and finish it. If you don't have the discipline to stick to it on your own, find a friend who will hold you accountable. Pick an honest person who will have the boldness to say, *"It's been a few days and I've noticed you haven't read the Bible….what's going on?"* Trust me, this level of accountability helps!

Do whatever it takes to stick to your plan and become familiar with God's voice!

#7 Just Do It!

All of the moments I have recounted in this book of God leading me and guiding me in His calling only took place because I made the effort to spend dedicated alone time with God. Often God spoke these things to me when, honestly, I wasn't asking about them or even thinking about them. I was just spending time with Him.

The truth is that we never really know what will come out of our time alone with God. The possibilities are endless! Yet, we will never know if we aren't making the time.

That's why today, I want to encourage you…make the time.

Don't believe the lie that prayer and Bible reading are optional. Don't fall for the trap that ignoring these spiritual disciplines is no big deal.

Instead, today, recognize your need to be familiar with the voice of God and begin making prayer and Bible reading a priority in your life.

Do whatever it takes to incorporate these disciplines in your life so that when God speaks to you, you'll be able to recognize His voice and follow Him.

Group Study Questions:

1. What does it mean to be *"familiar"* with the voice of God?

2. How do we develop this familiarity?

3. Do you have a set time to get alone with God to hear His voice?

4. What is one thing you can sacrifice to spend time alone with God?

5. Where do you spend time with God? How do you avoid distractions?

6. After reading this chapter, what is one thing you will put into practice or one thing you will change in your life?

7. How can we as a group help you do this?

Radical Challenge:

Sit down and create a plan to spend time with God. Decide:

When is the best time for you to read the Bible and pray?

Where is the best place?

Who do you need to share your plan with so you won't be interrupted?

Are there other distractions (like your phone or computer) that you need to remove from your prayer time?

What Bible reading plan will you do?

Once you've created a plan—start doing it every day. If you need accountability, who will help you stick to your commitment?

Chapter Five

Connecting To Your Power Source

But you will receive power when the Holy Spirit comes on you; and you will be my witnesses in Jerusalem, and in all Judea and Samaria, and to the ends of the earth.
(Acts 1:8, NIV)

They were just twelve ordinary men.

A few fishermen. A few Zealots.

A tax collector and one guy who seriously struggled with doubt.

None of them had much education or influence. They didn't come from a priestly line and they certainly weren't kings!

The only thing they had going for them was that each one answered Jesus' call when He said, *"Follow Me,"* and then they spent the next three years of their lives doing exactly that.

For three years, they traveled with Jesus. They listened to Him speak. They saw the miracles—-the sick who were healed, the demon possessed delivered. They collected the baskets full of bread after Jesus fed both the 4,000 and the 5,000. They were even there to see Lazarus walk out of his tomb when He came back from the dead.

They heard all of Jesus' public teaching and were even privy to private teaching that no one else heard.

They ate the Last Supper.

They were at the crucifixion and encountered the resurrected Jesus.

These twelve ordinary men had front row tickets to it all.

Now it was their turn to fulfill their calling by accepting the Great Commission and being the ones who would begin the effort to ***"Go into all the world and preach the Gospel to all creation." (Mark 16:15, NIV)***

But first, they had to do one thing.

Because even after all of the time they spent with Jesus, even after all they saw, all they experienced, and all of the things Jesus taught them, Jesus knew they still weren't able to fulfill the call God placed on their lives alone. So He gave them these instructions:

> ***On one occasion, while he was eating with them, he gave them this command:***
>
> ***"Do not leave Jerusalem, but wait for the gift my Father promised, which you have heard me speak about.***
>
> ***For John baptized with water, but in a few days you will be baptized with the Holy Spirit.....***
>
> ***...But you will receive power when the Holy Spirit comes***

on you;

and you will be my witnesses in Jerusalem, and in all Judea and Samaria, and to the ends of the earth." (Acts 1:4-5 and 8, NIV)

Of course, this wasn't the first time Jesus spoke to His disciples about the Holy Spirit. He'd been getting them ready for the moment He would return to Heaven even before He died.

John 14:16-18 and 25-27 (NIV) says:

I will ask the Father, and he will give you another advocate to help you and be with you forever—the Spirit of truth.

The world cannot accept him, because it neither sees him nor knows him.

But you know him, for he lives with you and will be in you.

I will not leave you as orphans; I will come to you.

All this I have spoken while still with you.

But the Advocate, the Holy Spirit, whom the Father will send in my name, will teach you all things and will remind you of everything I have said to you.

Peace I leave with you; my peace I give you. I do not give to you as the world gives. Do not let your hearts be troubled and do not be afraid.

These verses are so special because they showed the disciples (and us) some of the ways that the Holy Spirit would work in their lives. Specifically, we see that while Jesus walked alongside the disciples, the Holy Spirit would always be with them, because He would live inside of them.

Jesus also shows the very important way that the Holy Spirit would help them walk in their God-given calling: He would teach them all things and remind them of everything Jesus said to them.

Later, in John 15:26-27, Jesus continued teaching the disciples about the Holy Spirit when He said:

> *When the Advocate comes, whom I will send to you from the Father—the Spirit of truth who goes out from the Father—he will testify about me.*
>
> *And you also must testify, for you have been with me from the beginning. (NIV)*

> **The Holy Spirit would teach them all things and remind them of everything Jesus said to them.**

In this verse, we see Jesus continuing to teach them that their job to testify about all that they had seen and learned from Jesus would require that they be filled with the Holy Spirit.

Later He tells them:

> *But now I am going away to the one who sent me, and not one of you is asking where I am going.*
>
> *Instead, you grieve because of what I've told you.*
>
> *But in fact, it is best for you that I go away, because if I don't, the Advocate won't come. If I do go away, then I will send him to you.*
>
> *And when he comes, he will convict the world of its sin, and of God's righteousness, and of the coming judgment.....*
>
> *...There is so much more I want to tell you, but you can't bear it now.*

> *When the Spirit of truth comes, he will guide you into all truth. He will not speak on his own but will tell you what he has heard. He will tell you about the future.*
>
> *He will bring me glory by telling you whatever he receives from me.*
>
> *All that belongs to the Father is mine; this is why I said, "The Spirit will tell you whatever he receives from me." (John 16:5-8 and 12-15, NLT)*

Now the time had come. The moment they were dreading, the moment Jesus would leave and return to Heaven had arrived. But, as He promised, He did not leave them alone. It was time for their Advocate, the Spirit of Truth, the Comforter, to come. Just as Jesus commanded them, they were all meeting together in one place in Jerusalem.

> *When the day of Pentecost came, they were all together in one place.*
>
> *Suddenly a sound like the blowing of a violent wind came from heaven and filled the whole house where they were sitting.*
>
> *They saw what seemed to be tongues of fire that separated and came to rest on each of them.*
>
> *All of them were filled with the Holy Spirit and began to speak in other tongues as the Spirit enabled them. (Acts 2:1-4, NIV)*

This was no hidden event! Nope, people from all over Jerusalem began to notice.

> *Now there were staying in Jerusalem God-fearing Jews from every nation under heaven.*

> *When they heard this sound, a crowd came together in bewilderment, because each one heard their own language being spoken.*
>
> *Utterly amazed, they asked: "Aren't all these who are speaking Galileans? Then how is it that each of us hears them in our native language?*
>
> *Parthians, Medes and Elamites; residents of Mesopotamia, Judea and Cappadocia, Pontus and Asia, Phrygia and Pamphylia, Egypt and the parts of Libya near Cyrene; visitors from Rome (both Jews and converts to Judaism); Cretans and Arabs—we hear them declaring the wonders of God in our own tongues!"*
>
> *Amazed and perplexed, they asked one another, "What does this mean?" (Acts 2:5-12, NIV)*

One of the most telling lines in this verse is: *"Aren't all these who are speaking Galileans?"* Why is this so important? Well, it wasn't exactly a compliment.

Instead, it's important to understand that the people of Jerusalem looked down on the people from Galilee. The people from Jerusalem believed they were the elite, the sophisticated, the educated, and influential. They viewed the people of Galilee as their crazy, hillbilly cousins from the North. *"Galilean—Fool"* was one of the people of Jerusalem's favorite sayings. In today's language, the affluent, hoity-toity establishment Jerusalemites would call them the *"Deplorables."*

When it comes to the topic of languages, Alfred Edersheim says,

"There was a general contempt in Rabbinic circles for all that was Galilean. They even hated the way the people of Galilee spoke. Although the Judean or Jerusalem dialect was far from pure, the people of Galilee were especially blamed for neglecting the study of their language, charged with errors in grammar, and especially with absurd mispronunciation,

sometimes leading to ridiculous mistakes." [1]

So basically, the people who were listening to the disciples speak under the power of the Holy Spirit were saying, *"What is going on??? How do these hicks even know our languages…let alone how are they speaking them correctly? What is happening here?"*

That's when the Holy Spirit empowered Peter, the man who was formerly too afraid to admit that he even knew Jesus at the cross, to stand up in front of the massive crowd and begin walking in his calling.

> *Then Peter stood up with the Eleven, raised his voice and addressed the crowd:*
>
> *"Fellow Jews and all of you who live in Jerusalem, let me explain this to you; listen carefully to what I say*
>
> *These people are not drunk, as you suppose. It's only nine in the morning!*
>
> *No, this is what was spoken by the prophet Joel:*
>
> *'In the last days, God says,*
>   *I will pour out my Spirit on all people.*
> *Your sons and daughters will prophesy,*
>   *your young men will see visions,*
>   *your old men will dream dreams.*
> *Even on my servants, both men and women,*
>   *I will pour out my Spirit in those days,*
>   *and they will prophesy.*
> *I will show wonders in the heavens above*
>   *and signs on the earth below,*
>   *blood and fire and billows of smoke.*
> *The sun will be turned to darkness*
>   *and the moon to blood*
>   *before the coming of the great and glorious day of the*

> *Lord.*
> *And everyone who calls*
>   *on the name of the Lord will be saved.'*
>
> *Fellow Israelites, listen to this: Jesus of Nazareth was a man accredited by God to you by miracles, wonders and signs, which God did among you through him, as you yourselves know.*
>
> *This man was handed over to you by God's deliberate plan and foreknowledge; and you, with the help of wicked men, put him to death by nailing him to the cross.*
>
> *But God raised him from the dead, freeing him from the agony of death, because it was impossible for death to keep its hold on him." (Acts 2:14-24, NIV)*

The Holy Spirit brought the boom in and through Peter! Talk about empowerment! Just as Jesus had promised, when the disciples were baptized in the Holy Spirit, they were filled with boldness and able to walk in their calling. As promised, when Peter was put in front of a crowd of people, the Holy Spirit gave him the words to speak. He reminded Peter of all that Jesus had taught him. He empowered Peter to deliver the bold message that the people listening, the people who were looking down on him and calling him a *"Galilean,"* must repent and accept Jesus as the Messiah.

The results:

> *Those who accepted his message were baptized, and about three thousand were added to their number that day. (Acts 2:41, NIV)*

Three thousand people accepted Jesus and were baptized in one day! This was only the beginning! As we continue to read through the book of Acts, we continue to see all of the disciples, and later Paul, changing the world with the message of the Gospel through the empowerment of the Holy Spirit.

Through the Holy Spirit, we see them perform miracles.

We see unexplainable boldness even in the face of persecution and martyrdom.

Best of all, we see twelve ordinary men with no special abilities, education, or training, walking in their calling and changing their world with the Gospel of Jesus.

You might say, *"Well, that's awesome....but what does it matter to me?"*

Here's how it matters to you: **This same Holy Spirit that filled and empowered these twelve ordinary men from Galilee wants to empower you to walk in your calling and fulfill your God-given purpose in life.**

Acts 2:39 says, *"The promise (the gift of the Holy Spirit) is for you and your children and for all who are far off—for all whom the Lord our God will call." (NIV)*

You see, the promise of the baptism in the Holy Spirit and the empowerment it brings into our lives didn't end after the last chapter of the New Testament was written. No, this promise continues for today and tomorrow. It is a gift that gives everyone that God has called the empowerment to walk in their calling.

"But doesn't this just apply to people who are called into full-time vocational ministry: pastors, evangelists, missionaries?"

Absolutely not!

As we've talked about in a previous chapter, **EVERYONE** who has been born again and become a part of God's family, has a role to play in God's kingdom. Just like the twelve disciples, each one of us needs the baptism in the Holy Spirit and the empowerment that it brings enabling us to walk in our calling and fulfill it. It is how we go from just ordinary people to people who can change and influence the world around us for the kingdom of God.

Because the Holy Spirit is always with you, living inside of you, He can empower you in every area of your life.

The empowerment of the Holy Spirit will help you in your relationships. It will make you a better parent and spouse, child, sibling, friend, and neighbor.

> **The empowerment of the Holy Spirit is how we go from just ordinary people to people who can change and influence the world around us for the kingdom of God.**

It will make you a better worker in your vocation.

The Holy Spirit will give you the right words to say as you are interacting with people.

His empowerment will help you through difficult circumstances, giving you boldness, courage, peace, and wisdom.

The empowerment of the Holy Spirit will help you discern truth from lies. (Who doesn't need that in today's society?)

It will make you sensitive to sin as you will feel the conviction of the Holy Spirit telling you, *"This doesn't please God, stop it."*

Probably most importantly, the empowerment that comes from the baptism in the Holy Spirit will give you the boldness to be a witness for God, a person who shares the good news about Jesus with everyone in their sphere of influence with both their words and their lifestyle.

It is a gift given to us by God that enables us to live every part of our lives better. This enables us to reach our full potential in our God-given calling. Just like the twelve ordinary men, we cannot do it alone…that's why Jesus gave us the Holy Spirit.

"But isn't this just a Pentecostal thing?"

No, it's a Jesus thing.

Jesus introduced the disciples to the Holy Spirit. He told them to go to Jerusalem and wait for the baptism in the Holy Spirit. God offers every believer the baptism in the Holy Spirit so that they can fully walk in their calling and experience all of the benefits that the Holy Spirit brings.

This brings us to this chapter's radical challenge: It is the responsibility of every believer to seek the baptism of the Holy Spirit. After we have received it, we are responsible to be active in our prayer language on a consistent basis.

If you have not previously received the baptism in the Holy Spirit, I encourage you to start praying and asking God for it today. Whenever an opportunity is given to receive the baptism in the Holy Spirit at a church service, a conference, or even a prayer meeting, go forward to the altar and ask for it.

I went to the altar many times before I eventually was filled with the Holy Spirit. I remember the night it happened. I was a freshman in Bible College. For years, my mom would drag me to the altar every time there was an altar call for the baptism in the Holy Spirit. Struggling a bit with rebellion at this time of my life, I only went because she made me and I did it in a defiant attitude. Of course, I was never filled seeking this way.

As I got older, I began honestly going forward wanting it, and the first few times, I didn't receive it. Then a few weeks into my freshman year at the University of Valley Forge, they had what was called *"Spiritual Enrichment"* week, which meant they had evening services on top of the daily chapels. I remember in that day's chapel, the speaker said, *"Come tonight expecting the baptism in the Holy Spirit."*

I remember all day long I just knew that was the night I would be baptized. I remember walking to the service with a friend and saying, *"I'm getting filled tonight."* When the altar call came, I leapt up and was one of the first to get to the altar. (I always sat in the back, still do, and it took me longer to get there. Shout out to all my fellow back-row sitters!)

I remember the speaker laying hands on me, and the next thing I knew I was flat on my back on the floor! I had been slain in the Spirit. I was laying there speaking in tongues!

Not only that, after the initial speaking in tongues, I began laughing out loud. As someone who had lived in a lot of emotional and physical pain and who struggled with moodiness and depression, I guess God figured I need a little of the joy of the Lord. I felt so happy, but more importantly, I left that service filled with the Spirit!

I tell you this story to encourage you that, even if you don't receive the baptism in the Holy Spirit the first time you ask, keep seeking it. Keep going forward to the altar. Keep asking for it during your prayer time. (Because you can be filled with the Holy Spirit in your prayer closet as well as in a church.) Don't give up if it doesn't happen right away.

Remember: the disciples were seeking God, waiting together in Jerusalem for the Holy Spirit. When it was God's time (the day of Pentecost), they were filled with the Spirit and empowered. Until God gave them the gift, they were obedient in their responsibility to wait in Jerusalem and pray. You can follow their example by consistently praying and asking for the baptism in the Holy Spirit.

In the meantime, as you pray, I encourage you to read Tim

Enlow's book, *"Want More? Experience Greater Spiritual Intimacy and Power Through the Holy Spirit Baptism"* to learn more about the baptism in the Holy Spirit and how it will benefit your life.

What if you have already been baptized in the Holy Spirit?

You, too, have a responsibility because the baptism in the Holy Spirit isn't a one time experience. Instead, it is a gift that is supposed to be active in our lives every single day, empowering us to do what God has called us to do.

The question each of us has to answer is *"Are we regularly stirring up the gift God has given?"*

Recently, I heard Pastor Don Immel, the Penndel District Superintendent, say at the Penndel Ministry Summit:

"If we are going to be spiritually healthy, we must be in the Word and prayer. If we are going to be healthy Pentecostals…then we should also be active in our prayer language on a consistent basis…are we full of the Spirit or not?"

I have to admit that when I heard this it really convicted me. Because even though I was baptized in the Holy Spirit twenty-five years ago and I've used my prayer language throughout my life, I realized that I hadn't been making it a daily discipline in my life. This statement made me rethink my application of this gift. Since then, I have made it a priority that every day I spend at least five minutes using my prayer language.

Why?

Because I realize that just like the twelve disciples, without the empowerment and anointing of the Holy Spirit, I am nothing. Without Him, I am unable to fulfill God's calling in my life.

So I've become pro-active about stirring up the gift and daily praying in tongues. Again, this principle doesn't just apply to pastors—-it is for everyone who wants to walk in their God-given calling. Just as we said that every calling comes with responsibilities, one of our responsibilities is to embrace the baptism in the Holy Spirit and the empowerment it brings.

It starts by seeking the baptism in the Holy Spirit.

Once we are baptized in the Holy Spirit, we need to be actively using our prayer language and stirring up the gift that God has given us.

Rather than taking this amazing gift that God has offered us for granted, we need to embrace it and take advantage of all that it has to offer us.

This is how we….just ordinary people…can change our world for God: through the empowerment of the Holy Spirit.

Group Study Questions:

1. This chapter talked about how the baptism in the Holy Spirit changed the lives of the disciples—share what their stories mean to you.

2. Why is it important to be filled with the Spirit to fulfill the Great Commission?

3. Have you been baptized in the Holy Spirit? Share your testimony.

4. Why do you think some people are filled immediately while others take more time?

5. Do you regularly use your prayer language?

6. After reading this chapter, what is one thing you will put into practice or one thing you will change in your life?

7. How can we as a group help you do this?

Radical Challenge:

This chapter said: *"It is the responsibility of every believer to seek the baptism of the Holy Spirit. After we have received it, we are responsible to be active in our prayer language consistently."*

Are you accepting your responsibility?

If you are not baptized in the Holy Spirit, commit to seeking this gift today.

If you have been baptized in the Holy Spirit, commit to using your prayer language each day.

Chapter Six
Taking The Leap

Now faith is confidence in what we hope for and assurance about what we do not see.
(Hebrews 11:1, NIV)

It was the summer of 2013. After a spring of traveling to women's ministry events serving Adessa at her table and being her assistant, I was absolutely sure that the Holy Spirit was showing me the need for similar events designed to minister to men. I KNEW it was God's will, and I talked to Adessa about it for months. It seemed that everywhere we turned, we were receiving confirmations that this was God's will.

Yet, we were unsure how to overcome two major issues that at the time seemed insurmountable.

First, there were the issues of insecurity and fear. I mean, no one was asking me to do these events. I was well aware that it was totally out of my place to suggest they needed to be done, let alone offer to lead them. Fear of rejection, failure, and not wanting to offend those in leadership made me think that God needed to share this vision with someone with more experience.

The other major obstacle was money. Mostly, we didn't have any. Following God's call to hold conferences would mean that we had to invest the minuscule personal emergency fund we'd worked so hard to save. If nobody came to the events or something happened in our personal lives, financially, we were sunk.

So I did nothing. Until one evening when we were live-streaming an evening session of the Assemblies of God General Council Service and Pastor Choco was speaking. When he said, *"If you are too afraid to do what God has called you to do, you don't even belong in ministry,"* I felt like someone stabbed me in the chest! That same night, I called the head of our district's Mens Ministry, a man who at the time terrified me because of my fears and issues of abuse in my past, and made an appointment to talk about starting Mantour Ministries.

Over the next few weeks, we took a leap of faith and once again followed God's call out of simple obedience. They were the first steps of faith that led to me walking in God's call for our lives—but what frightening steps they were at the time.

Adessa and I felt very much like Abraham when he packed his bags and followed God into a new land without knowing where he was going or the twelve disciples who chose to follow Jesus not knowing where it would lead. All we knew was that God said *"Go"* and we chose to follow and let the rest to Him.

Of course, this wasn't the first time God asked us to follow Him and take a leap of faith, and there have been many more leaps since. Each one has reinforced to me the Biblical truth that if you want to walk in God's calling for your life one of the requirements is faith.

Throughout my life, one of my favorite passages of Scripture has been Hebrews 11. Many call it the *'Hall of Fame Of Faith.'* As you read through each verse, you can once again see that anyone who has ever made a significant impact on the kingdom of God and walked in the fullness of their calling has at some point in their lives had to choose to have faith.

Abel built an acceptable altar.

Noah built a boat when it never even rained.

Abraham left his hometown without knowing where he was going.

Joseph believed God would rescue the children of Israel.

Moses' parents disobeyed the law and saved his life.

Moses went back to Egypt, risking his life, believing that God would set the Israelites free.

Rahab helped the Israelites spies and trusted that she would be saved when she put the red cord in her window.

On and on the list goes of men and women of faith who made choices that did not make sense. They obeyed God even when the outcome was uncertain, simply because they had faith that God told them to do it.

We look at these people as the *"all-stars of the Bible"*, but the reality is that the only difference between them and us is that we already know the outcome of their leaps of faith, whereas we are living in real-time.

Their lives are given to us as examples that we are to follow. Because the idea of following God in faith didn't end with the New Testament. Instead, it continues today as God continues to ask people to step outside of their comfort zone, to take risks, to go places, and do things, trusting solely that He has called them to do it.

The challenge that stands before each of us is *"Are we willing to be people of faith?"*

Being completely honest, I'll admit that it isn't always easy. I remember that I was literally shaking as I went to the meeting to share God's vision with the people who needed to approve it. I know Adessa was scared to death that I'd get blown out of the water and not recover!

When we had to put our tiny savings account on the line to pay for the start up costs, it was scary. In fact, Adessa told me *"We can plan four events. It's all we can afford and if we lose it all at least we won't have debt."* (By the way, we did seven events that year.)

When we announced the events, we had no idea what would happen. Would anyone come? Did men want conferences designed for them? Would people get behind the idea or laugh us out of town? Would they say, *"Who is this guy and his sister?"* or would they take a chance and give this new idea a try?

> **The challenge that stands before each of us is "Are we willing to be people of faith?"**

These were the thoughts going through our minds as we took those first few steps of faith. So, yeah, I understand how hard it can be to blindly follow God. Yet, it isn't about how hard it is—-it's about obeying the One Who called you. As Hebrews 11:6 says:

> *And without faith it is impossible to please God, because anyone who comes to him must believe that he exists and that he rewards those who earnestly seek him. (NIV)*

This is a powerful scripture that we need to consider as we are choosing whether or not we will follow God in faith.

It's this chapter's radical challenge: When deciding whether or not to take a step of faith we need to ask ourselves, *"Do I want to please God?"*

Do I want to walk in God's will for my life? Do I want my life to be marked by obedience or disobedience to God? These are real questions we need to consider. Because it isn't just about whether or not we are afraid or whether we want to do what God is asking. It's a matter of obedience and choosing to please God versus disobedience.

> **Faith means that because you believe God has told you to do something you do it with with all of the effort, passion, energy, and strength that you have.**

Of course, while we're talking about faith, we need to make one point very clear: it isn't enough to just blindly take a leap and trust God to make magic happen.

There's a quote, supposedly by St. Augustine, that says, *"Pray as though everything depended on God; act as though everything depended on you."*

James says it differently when he says, **"You foolish person, do you want evidence that faith without deeds is useless?" (James 2:20, NIV)**

One of the biggest mistakes that too many Christians make is they confuse *"faith"* with *"laziness"*. The two are far from synonymous. Instead, faith means that because you believe God has told you to do something you do it with with all of the effort, passion, energy, and strength that you have.

For instance, Noah didn't just wait for a boat to appear. No, he gathered his sons and they worked for years building a boat.

Moses didn't wait for the Pharaoh to summon him from Egypt to rescue the people of Israel. Instead, he put his life on the line and went to Egypt to confront Pharaoh.

> **Living by faith doesn't remove our obligation to work. Instead, our faith should compel us to work harder because we believe that we are working for God.**

It's so important that we understand that living by faith doesn't remove our obligation to work. Instead, our faith should compel us to work harder because we believe that we are working for God. If we are working for God, then we should do the absolute best job that we can, trusting that as we partner with Him through our work, He will partner with us to produce the results.

Another thing we need to understand about faith is that it isn't just a one time thing. (Sorry to disappoint you.) Walking by faith isn't about one individual leap, but more of a lifetime of steps following God wherever He leads. One thing I've seen in our lives is that just about the time I take a deep breath and say, *"Wow! God came through. We followed Him in faith and He was faithful, now we can settle in for a less risky season of life,"* that's when the Holy Spirit starts asking us to take another step of faith.

For instance, right after our first Mantour season, the Holy Spirit began leading us to form a 501c3 non-profit organization combining the men's and women's ministries. (Again, a huge leap of faith and more money.)

Next, He challenged us to start writing books. Again, it was a leap of faith as we wondered if we could do it, how we could pay for it, and whether anyone would want to read them.

Then we started donating books to prisons.

Then the *"big step of faith"* (that made all the other steps seem small) came when the Holy Spirit opened the door for our ministry to come under the Assemblies of God US Missions.

Even this year, the Holy Spirit is leading us to once again follow Him in faith as I begin not just donating books to prisons, but ministering in prisons. Then there was perhaps our biggest challenge yet, as the Holy Spirit led us to take a step of faith and build dedicated office space for the ministry. Compared to this project, that little investment we made into those first few conferences seems small.

Yet, it's all the same commitment.

Jesus says, ***"Follow Me in faith"*** and we say **"Whatever it takes."**

Today, the question I have for you is: *"What step of faith is God asking you to take to walk in your calling?"*

Because the principle of living a life of faith doesn't just apply to people in ministry.

Instead, the man who God is leading to spend more time with his family may need to pass on that big promotion he has been pursuing because it would require longer hours at the office.

At the same time, God may be asking another man to leave his hometown to take a job in a distant city. That will take a step of faith.

Some are called to adopt, become foster parents, or a mentor.

Others are called to start their own business or volunteer in their community.

Maybe God's asking you to teach a class in your church or go talk to a neighbor about Jesus.

The possibilities are endless, but the question remains the same. When God tells you to take a step of faith, will you obey?

Are you willing to say, *"WHATEVER IT TAKES, I will follow You?"*

Even as you say those words are you willing to put in the effort needed on your part to partner with God to see your step of faith come to fruition?

Do you want to live a life of faith or fear?

Ultimately, the choice is up to you.

Do you want to live a life of faith that leads to you living in the calling God has for you?

An essential step is following God in faith.

Group Study Questions:

1. Why does God often require us to take leaps of faith when we walk in our calling?

2. Have you ever refused to take a leap of faith that God was asking you to do? What caused you to resist taking the leap?

3. What was the last leap of faith God called you to take?

4. What does the phrase *"Pray as though everything depended on God; act as though everything depended on you"* mean?

5. Do you want to live a life of faith or fear? How do you make your answer happen?

6. After reading this chapter, what is one thing you will put into practice or one thing you will change in your life?

7. How can we as a group help you do this?

Radical Challenge:

This chapter says: *"When deciding whether or not to take a step of faith we need to ask ourselves, 'Do I want to please God?'"*

What step of faith is God asking you to take to walk in your calling?

How can you walk in obedience?

Recognize the first step you need to take and then take it.

Chapter Seven
The Price Is Right

Again, the Kingdom of Heaven can be illustrated by the story of a man going on a long trip. He called together his servants and entrusted his money to them while he was gone. He gave five bags of silver to one, two bags of silver to another, and one bag of silver to the last—dividing it in proportion to their abilities. He then left on his trip.

The servant who received the five bags of silver began to invest the money and earned five more. The servant with two bags of silver also went to work and earned two more. But the servant who received the one bag of silver dug a hole in the ground and hid the master's money.

After a long time their master returned from his trip and called them to give an account of how they had used his money. The servant to whom he had entrusted the five bags of silver came forward with five more and said, "Master, you gave me five bags of silver to invest, and I have earned five more."

The master was full of praise. "Well done, my good and faithful servant. You have been faithful in handling this small amount, so now I will give you many more responsibilities. Let's celebrate together!"

The servant who had received the two bags of silver came forward and said, "Master, you gave me two bags of silver to invest, and I have earned two more."

The master said, "Well done, my good and faithful servant. You have been faithful in handling this small amount, so now I will give you many more responsibilities. Let's celebrate together!"

Then the servant with the one bag of silver came and said, "Master, I knew you were a harsh man, harvesting crops you didn't plant and gathering crops you didn't cultivate. I was afraid I would lose your money, so I hid it in the earth. Look, here is your money back."

But the master replied, "You wicked and lazy servant! If you knew I harvested crops I didn't plant and gathered crops I didn't cultivate, why didn't you deposit my money in the bank? At least I could have gotten some interest on it."

Then he ordered, "Take the money from this servant, and give it to the one with the ten bags of silver."

(Matthew 25:14-28, NLT)

I've heard the story so many times that it almost doesn't surprise me anymore. (Although I have to admit that it still makes me a little sad every time I hear it.)

Someone comes to us all excited. They were at a special event or a Mantour Conference and the Holy Spirit spoke to them, giving them direction for their lives. Over the next few weeks, they've had confirmations that it was the Holy Spirit speaking to them and they couldn't be more pumped. They simply cannot wait to share everything that is in their heart as they prepare to follow God's direction in their life.

Then the story begins to change as they begin exploring the responsibilities or steps necessary to follow God's path for their life. Quickly, their enthusiasm takes a nosedive.

For instance, there was the woman who was thrilled when the Holy Spirit confirmed to her that it was time for her to once again pursue the calling God had spoken over her life when she was a little girl. Unfortunately, some things had happened in her life and she felt like her calling was lost forever. Yet, one day as she answered an altar call, she was sure she heard God say that He still had a plan for her life and He wanted her to begin moving forward in her calling again.

Over the next few weeks, she was given several confirmations that this was God's will for her life. Filled with excitement, she started down the road to follow her calling. Everything was great until she found out that she needed to take some classes. The classes cost money and she didn't want to make the financial investment. Instead, she decided to go on vacation. And that is the end of the story.

Of course, money isn't always the issue. I knew a guy who felt that God was calling him to take the exact same classes. He signed up for the class, investing a good amount of money into the fee, and then quit halfway through because of a disagreement with a classmate. This minor personality clash was more of an issue for him than obeying God and walking in his calling.

Then there was the gentleman who invested both the money and the time into taking the classes he needed to follow God's call on his life. However, he got sidelined when he found out that he would have to give up drinking alcohol to become an Assemblies of God minister. Despite all the time and money he put in, he just couldn't make this sacrifice. Instead, he walked away from the whole idea.

Sadly, these are just a few stories I could tell. Every time I see another person make a similar choice in life, I think of Mark 10 where a rich young man approached Jesus and asked how he could be a part of God's kingdom and inherit eternal life. When Jesus asked him to make an investment greater than he was willing to sacrifice, he walked away sad realizing that to him, following Jesus just wasn't worth it.

At this point you might be saying, *"C'mon, that's a little harsh. I mean Jesus asked the young man to sell all of his possessions and give them to the poor. That's a big ask."*

And yet, if we think about it, it's the same thing Jesus asked of the twelve disciples when He said, **"Come, Follow Me and I will send you out to fish for people." (Matthew 4:19, NIV)**

The disciples made the choice the rich young ruler would not make when they walked away from it all to follow Jesus. They realized that the kingdom of God is worth everything. It is the hidden treasure and the pearl of great price.

> ***The kingdom of heaven is like treasure hidden in a field. When a man found it, he hid it again, and then in his joy went and sold all he had and bought that field.***
>
> ***Again, the kingdom of heaven is like a merchant looking for fine pearls. When he found one of great value, he went away and sold everything he had and bought it. (Matthew 13:44-46, NIV)***

Even though it cost them everything, the disciples chose to follow Jesus. Today, they set the example for all of us as we come to terms with the radical truth that fulfilling God's call for your life requires investment. Seeing a vision become a reality requires sacrifice. Whether or not you are willing to endure and embrace this truth often determines whether or not you will see God's vision for your life fulfilled.

I know that's hard to hear, but it's the truth: There's no guarantee that you are going to fulfill God's purpose for your life. No, you can only fulfill God's purpose for your life when you are willing to submit to God's process for your life. Often this process involves making an investment.

The hard truth is that fulfilling God's call for your life isn't magical. You don't just have an experience at an altar and then *"poof"*, you are walking in your calling.

Nope. Sorry. Not gonna happen.

Instead, anyone who is actively following God's plan and purpose for their lives will tell you that their journey included the choice to make personal sacrifices and investments. They worked hard. They prayed hard. They went without things. They cried. They struggled. They put time into learning and growing. The life you may be admiring today didn't come easy…instead, it took blood, sweat, and tears.

> **Seeing a vision become a reality requires a lot of sacrifice. Whether or not you are willing to endure and embrace this truth often determines whether or not you will see God's vision for your life fulfilled.**

Of course, most of them will also tell you that it was worth everything they invested as they are now reaping the dividends and seeing God work in and through their lives.

So what are some of the investments that need to be made to follow God's call on your life?

Investment in Learning

No matter what path God has called you to follow in life, the odds are that you will need to invest in learning how to do it. If it's a calling into a vocation, you will probably need to go to school or take some form of classes. Thankfully, due to technology, there are now a variety of options available for how to gain an education. Whereas years ago, a person who felt that God was calling them into full-time ministry would have needed to quit their job and move their family to a Bible college, today, you can take courses online or attend a local school of ministry.

The same is true if God is calling you into a particular secular vocation. For instance, my friend's wife spent the first twenty years of their marriage homeschooling her children. After they graduated, she felt that God was calling her to get her master's degree in science. She obeyed and took all of her courses online. Today, God is using her to write advanced homeschooling math and science curriculums that are being used around the world.

Of course, a choice to invest in learning doesn't just apply to our vocations. Instead, investing in learning reaps dividends in all areas of life, including our relationships.

For instance, our Mom did not come from a happy family. There were a lot of problems and she had a very unhappy childhood. One of her goals in life was to give us a better life than she had. After she came to God, she started reading every book on parenting that she could get her hands on. She invested her time and money into learning and put what she learned into practice. Because of her investment, Adessa and I have a totally different testimony than either of our parents. Her goal was met because she invested in learning.

An investment in education and learning is never wasted.

Will it take sacrifice? Absolutely.

However, the sacrifice will pay dividends when God can use your investment to produce results for His kingdom.

Investment of Time

Obviously, the investment in learning is going to require an investment of time. It takes time to read, to study, to go to a class, and to learn. However, this is not the only way that following God's call on your life will require you to invest your time.

As we said before, following God's call on your life requires you to invest in prayer and Bible reading. Simply put: you can't follow someone unless you are familiar with their voice and the only way to become familiar with God's voice is by spending time with Him. What many people don't realize is that spending time with God is an investment. The dividends come in the form of a rich relationship with God and the anointing of the Holy Spirit on your life.

As our friend Lori Cullen says, *"You can't walk in the anointing of the Holy Spirit if you aren't spending time with Him."*

Many people say, *"I'm not a full-time minister, I don't need an anointing on my life."*

All I want to answer is: *"Are you kidding me?"*

"You don't need the Holy Spirit walking with you through your day, making your sharper, bolder, giving you strength, helping you to discern truth and lies, to do your job better, to love your family better, to be more Christ-like, to be a better representation of God on the earth? You don't need the empowerment of the Holy Spirit to live this life and walk in the calling God has for you? Of course, you do!!!"

That's why it's so important that we invest in spending time with God.

Another way that God calls us to invest in the kingdom of God is by serving others. Again, this takes sacrifice. It means giving up time we could spend doing things that we want to do to plant a seed in someone else's life for the kingdom of God. Whether it be volunteering in children's ministry, serving as an usher or on an evangelistic team, going on a missions trip or helping clean the bathrooms in the church, when we invest our time in service, God can produce a dividend for His kingdom.

Yet, so many people don't want to take the time to do the work God has called them to do.

They know God is calling them to mentor teens, but who has the time?

They believe God wants them to talk to their neighbors about God, but they are just so busy.

Then there is the all too common trap of *"someday."*

"Someday I'm going to take that trip."

"Someday I'm going to write that book and share my testimony."

"Someday I'm going to take that step of faith and lead the team."

And yet, too often, *"someday"* is just a way of avoiding their calling. Rather than investing the time necessary to fully walk in their calling and follow God's plan for their lives, they just keep putting it off. If I had a dollar for every time someone has told me, *"I really feel God calling me to write a book"* but then they never follow through and actually write it, I'd be able to go on a nice vacation on a beach with a fast jet ski at my disposal to jump the waves! What I've seen far too often is that *"someday"* eventually turns into never.

Instead, of waiting until *"someday"* to invest the time to do what God has called you to do, you need to obey the instructions in Hebrews and start investing the time to follow God's call on your life today. (Hebrews 3:13) Remember, tomorrow isn't promised, but there is still the opportunity to invest today into following God's plan for your life.

Investment of Finances

One of the biggest excuses that people make for why they can't follow God's plan for their lives is: *"I don't have the money. It's too expensive."*

Trust me, I've heard it all my life as an excuse for everything from why people can't obey God and tithe, to why they can't take a step of faith and follow God's call on their life.

And yet, while I am a big—I mean tremendous—-believer in proper money management, living on a budget, staying out of debt and saving money, my Mom also raised us to believe that there is no greater financial investment that we can make than investing in the kingdom of God.

When God calls us to do something, I don't believe we can just say, *"I can't afford it"* without investigating every possible avenue to see if it is possible to obey. We need to look at our finances and ask, *"Is there anything I can sacrifice? Where can I cut back? If God asked me to do this, then there must be a way to pay for it."* Then do all you can to find it.

As we said in the last chapter, throughout our lives, God has asked Adessa and me to make these types of investments over and over again. Every step of faith we've ever taken has required not just an investment of learning how to do something new and a sacrifice of time, but over and over again, God has asked us to make a financial investment that required us to trust Him to provide.

Time and again, we have taken the leap and made the investment trusting that God will produce spiritual dividends beyond anything we can imagine. Looking back on the investments we've made, God has never disappointed us. Whenever we've made a spiritual investment, it has reaped divine rewards.

Why do we do it?

Because I don't want to look back on my life someday and wonder, *"What if?"*

More importantly, I don't want to stand before God someday and have to answer, *"Why didn't you invest the resources I gave you into My kingdom?"*

Instead, I want to someday hear, **"Well done, my good and faithful servant. You have been faithful in handling this small amount, so now I will give you many more responsibilities. Let's celebrate together!" (Matthew 25:21, NLT)**

Today, my radical challenge to you is: What call has God placed on your heart?

What is your dream? What do you believe God is asking you to do to advance His kingdom?

After you've answered that question, it's time to answer a more difficult one:

Are you willing to make the investment necessary to experience God's purpose in your life?

Let's dig a little deeper:

What about the sacrifice God is calling you to make?

I know from experience that no calling is fulfilled without sacrifice. What are you willing to sacrifice to see God's purpose and vision for your life completed?

Today, I hope that this chapter encourages you to make the right choice. I hope it helps you realize that the investment that may appear to be a disruption or interference on your journey toward the vision God has given you is a part of God's plan to fulfill His purpose in your life. It is part of the process.

The question you need to answer is: *"Is following God's call worth the investment?"*

Today, I pray that you will make the choice that we and so many of our friends are making—-to say that it doesn't matter the investment—-we want to fulfill God's purpose in our lives. Don't become a cautionary tale of what could have been. Instead, re-frame your perspective and see every investment and every sacrifice as an on-ramp on the road to your destiny.

Don't give up—-don't allow yourself to be detoured.

Determine in your heart that more than anything you want to experience God's purpose in your life and go after it with all that you have.

Whatever the investment, whatever the sacrifice, the vision God has placed in your heart IS worth the effort. Don't miss all God has for you because getting there is hard or inconvenient. Instead, stay the course and see God's call fulfilled in your life—whatever it takes.

Group Study Questions:

1. What is the cost of walking in your calling?

2. What will walking in your calling require you to sacrifice?

3. What class can you take or book can you read to gain more knowledge to walk in your calling?

4. This chapter stated: *"You can't walk in the anointing of the Holy Spirit if you aren't spending time with Him."* What does this mean in your life?

5. How can you overcome the *"somedays"* that attack you? What have you been putting off that you need to do?

6. Is God's call worth the investment?

7. After reading this chapter, what is one thing you will put into practice or one thing you will change in your life?

8. How can we as a group help you do this?

Radical Challenge:

Take a moment and ask yourself: *"What call has God placed on my heart? What is my dream? What do I believe God is asking me to do to advance His kingdom?"*

Write your answers down.

Now answer a more difficult question:

"What investments are necessary for me to fulfill my God-given call?"

"What sacrifices do I need to make?"

Again, write down these answers.

Write down three practical steps you can take to start making this investment.

Then, next to each practical step, challenge yourself by writing down a deadline for you to start taking the practical step.

Finally, do whatever it takes to start investing in following God's call on your life.

Chapter Eight
You Don't Know What You Don't Know

When pride comes, then comes disgrace, but with humility comes wisdom.
(Proverbs 11:2, NIV)

How often have you heard the term *"male pride?"* Men don't ask advice because they have their pride. They accept no charity or help because of their pride. Their pride keeps them from being open with their emotions and feelings.

Male pride is openly acknowledged and even celebrated as if it is a good thing. However, it isn't good. It is sin. No matter what your unique, individual calling in life may be, one of the biggest deterrents to walking in all that God has planned for you is pride.

Thinking you know everything.

Believing you know it all and don't need advice.

Seeing yourself as the answer to every problem.

Believing that you know more than anyone who has gone before you and you will be the one to show them all how it's done.

> **Pride makes us blindly unaware to all of the things that we don't know. It hides our weaknesses, our lack of experience, and our deep need to learn from others.**

Guaranteed, any or all of these attitudes will lead to a reality check as you realize that Proverbs 16:18 was right when it said, *"Pride goes before destruction, a haughty spirit before a fall." (NIV)*

Check out the way The Message Version translates this same verse:

> *First pride, then the crash—the bigger the ego, the harder the fall.*

Why is this so inevitable?

Pride makes us blindly unaware to all of the things that we don't know. It hides our weaknesses, our lack of experience, and our deep need to learn from others. History shows that anyone who lets pride have a place in their life will soon find themselves repeating the words of the young man in Proverbs who would not listen to the voice of wisdom and said:

> *"Oh, why didn't I do what they told me?*
>
> *Why did I reject a disciplined life?*
>
> *Why didn't I listen to my mentors,*
>
> *or take my teachers seriously?*
>
> *My life is ruined!*

I haven't one blessed thing to show for my life!"
(Proverbs 5:12-14, The Message)

Thankfully, there is another way: humility. I like to define it as the ability to admit that you don't know what you don't know. A willingness to admit that you need help, advice, and to learn how to walk in your calling from those who have gone before you. Because trust me, whatever path God is calling you to walk, there is someone who has walked a similar road who has years of experience that they could pass on to you.

A young father can benefit from another dad who has successfully raised children for God.

A guy can learn from someone who has already achieved success in his own career.

Starting your own business? Then you can learn from another entrepreneur.

Whether it be in our relationships, our work, ministry, volunteering, or any area of life, the benefits of a mentoring relationship are invaluable. This is a principle that both my sister and I have found to be true.

> **Humility is the ability to admit that you don't know what you don't know.**

For instance, I remember the spring before I felt God's call to begin Mantour Ministries. Adessa and I were both teaching Berean school of ministry classes at night. I LOVED teaching these classes. As part of the class, I decided to lead the men in the group to hold a men's event to fulfill the internship requirement.

It's important to understand that leading into this time in my life, God was trying to bring a mentor into my life. However, because of the abuse in my past, my fears and my insecurity, I was having none of it! I kept the man God was trying to bring into my life at arms' length. Although I told him about the upcoming event, I didn't seek his wisdom or advice.

Eventually, the day of the event came. Even though I and the men taking the class worked hard and put all that we had into the event, because of our inexperience, there were some obvious mistakes and issues. Of course, my potential mentor heard about each and every error.

Well, fast forward a few months to the meeting I told you about earlier where I went to share my vision of the Mantours with my potential mentor. Obviously, the earlier event held had to be discussed. One of the first things he said to me was, *"If you'd have come to me for advice, I could have told you what you were doing wrong. Are you ready to take my advice?"*

Honestly, I knew he was right. I knew what I didn't know. I knew I was unprepared to do what God was calling me to do, and I knew I needed his years of wisdom and experience in my life. So I immediately accepted his offer.

From that day forward, both my ministry and my relationship with this mentor changed—-mostly because my attitude changed. Rather than letting fear control me, I chose to put on an attitude of humility and say, *"I am ready to learn. Show me how to walk in my God-given calling and do men's ministry the best way possible."*

Of course, I am not the only one who had to learn to put on humility and accept the help of a mentor. I don't think I'll ever forget the day that I sat and listened to Adessa have a phone call with the mentor God brought into her life. She called Adessa on the phone and gently (or not so gently) said, *"I've been watching your teaching videos and I need to be honest with you about this: You either need to stop posting videos or get better at it because your videos are really bad.*

You Don't Know What You Don't Know

You're making yourself and the ministry look bad."

She didn't end there—-instead, she had a list of things that needed to be changed and improved to make the videos better if Adessa decided to go forward. It was a pretty long list.

Adessa had three choices:

She could quit making videos. (But that would mean abandoning something she believed God was calling her to do.)

She could get angry, cry, and stop talking to her mentor. (I've seen people do it.)

Or she could take her mentor's list to heart and make the necessary improvements.

Adessa humbly chose the last option. We bought the necessary equipment, I worked on improving my video editing/production skills, and Adessa worked really hard to improve her on-camera skills.

Guess what happened. As we faithfully made the changes, Adessa started receiving really positive feedback about her videos. Years later, when someone asked where Adessa learned to do videos so well, she had to laugh and say, *"It was after my mentor told me I was terrible at it."*

These are just two examples of how an attitude of humility and the influence of mentors have helped Adessa and I walk in our God-given calling. There are so many more I could tell. In the end, each story would only reinforce the truth of Proverbs 13:10 that **"Wisdom is found in those who take advice." (NIV)**

At this point you may be saying, **"I see the need for a mentor. I want to be humble and learn all that I can. How do I find a mentor and how do I make the most of the opportunity?"**

Here are some practical ways to implement these principles into your life:

1. Be open to the mentor that God brings into your life.

The first step in finding a mentor is praying and asking God to bring the right mentor into your life. I truly believe that since this is a prayer that God wants to hear, He will answer it and bring just the right person into your life.

That's where things get a little tricky, because God may not always bring you the mentor you imagined. I know that neither Adessa or I would have picked the people that God knew would be best for us. However, they turned out to be exactly who we needed. Over time, they became not only our mentors, but our closest and most trusted friends.

On the other hand, in the past both Adessa and I have asked people to mentor us who have declined. The best attitude to have when this happens is to avoid offense and accept it as God's will. If they were who you really needed, it would have worked out. Since it didn't, let God bring the right person into your life.

2. Be respectful of your mentor's time.

A good mentor will be a busy mentor. Because they are successful, they will have a lot of responsibilities to juggle. Their willingness to mentor you is a gift which you need to respect.

Some practical ways to do this are to be flexible and adjust your schedule to their schedule rather than the other way around. Go to them instead of asking them to come to you.

If you text them or call them and they don't get back to you right away, don't be offended or angry. Don't entertain thoughts like, *"They hate me or they don't care about me."* Instead, realize they have a life outside of you. Cut them some slack, be patient, and be merciful if they forget. Recognize that any time they give you is a blessing and make the most of it.

3. You need to be transparent.

Discipleship only works when you are open and honest about your struggles and issues. If you are not willing to admit you have problems or that you have areas you need help with, then the process is doomed. True discipleship can only happen when we are willing to not hold back and be totally open and honest. It is a cost some refuse to pay, but to be properly discipled, it is necessary.

4. Listen more; talk less.

A healthy mentoring relationship will contain a significant amount of talking. Yet, humility makes you want to listen more, knowing that you need their wisdom more than you need to impress them with how much you know (a sign of pride). So while, yes, you will have an opportunity to talk and share your heart, you need to remember that the real benefit for you comes from listening.

Finally, beyond a doubt, this is the most important tip for making the most of a mentoring relationship.

5. Don't expect a participation trophy.

Let's face it, we live in a world where everyone expects to be praised, told they are the best, and not succeeding is okay as long as you try your hardest. Everyone gets a participation trophy. But that's not reality, especially in a mentor relationship.

You can't expect your mentor to always be praising you, telling you how great you are, and accepting second best. A good mentor will be hard on you. They will teach you how to achieve greatness and they will demand greatness of you. They will expect nothing less.

You have to be thick-skinned and except their criticism. You have to not only allow them to be tough on you, but ask them to be.

"Iron sharpens iron" is a popular saying…but iron sharpening iron is not an easy thing. It requires abrasion, friction, force, and a host of other scientific stuff that I don't understand. (Hey, science was never my thing…I almost didn't graduate Bible college because it required a science class!) In order to fully take advantage of a mentor relationship, you have to be open to correction, criticism, and admonishment.

6. Take your mentor's advice.

Here is the bottom line honest truth I have learned from years of observing people in mentoring relationships:

If a mentor believes you are listening to their advice and implementing it in your life, they will continue making the investment. However, if after awhile, they start to see that you're not listening to them or following their advice, they will start to back away and find someone else who will produce a dividend on their investment of time, energy, and wisdom.

It sounds harsh, but it's true.

I've known too many guys who had the opportunity to be mentored by amazing men of God who squandered it by refusing to humbly follow their mentor's guidance. Pride had too strong of a root in their life and they thought they knew better. Instead of walking through the mentorship door that God opened for them, they ran away and badmouthed their mentor. Just like it says in Proverbs, their pride led to their fall and they crashed and burned before fulfilling the God-given calling on their life.

Please do not make this choice!

Instead, choose to put on humility.

When God brings a mentor into your life, respect them enough to listen to them. Simply put: Do what they tell you to do!

Guaranteed, taking their advice will benefit you. (I've learned that 98% of the time, mentors are right and following their advice will help you succeed. The other 2%, it usually just doesn't turn out as great as they thought it would, but it never hurts you.)

Even more, God will honor your humility. As 1 Peter 5:5-6 says:

> *In the same way, you who are younger, submit yourselves to your elders. All of you, clothe yourselves with humility toward one another, because,*
>
> *"God opposes the proud, but shows favor to the humble."*
>
> *Humble yourselves, therefore, under God's mighty hand, that he may lift you up in due time. (NIV)*

The truth of this chapter is: Do you want to succeed in your God-given calling? Ask God to bring a mentor into your life, listen to what they say, and take their advice.

As someone who has put this principle into action in my own life, I can tell you that it is a decision you will never regret.

Group Study Questions:

1. Why is humility so important to walking in our calling?

2. Do you have a mentor? How have they influenced your life?

3. Has God been trying to bring a mentor into your life, but you've been resisting? Really look at your life and see if you are missing a blessing.

4. Why should you be respectful of their time?

5. Why is it important to do what your mentor tells you to do?

6. This chapter talked about *"not expecting a participation trophy from your mentor."* It's a funny way to put it, but how should you properly respond to criticism?

7. After reading this chapter, what is one thing you will put into practice or one thing you will change in your life?

8. How can we as a group help you do this?

Radical Challenge:

Is God trying to bring a mentor into your life?

Really analyze yourself and ask, *"How can I gain the most from this relationship?"*

Look at the tips above and determine what attitudes in your heart need to change. What new attitudes need to be developed so that you can learn as much as you can from your mentor?

Make a list and then start making the changes.

Chapter Nine
Higher Standards

So you must live as God's obedient children.
Don't slip back into your old ways of living to satisfy your own desires.
You didn't know any better then.
But now you must be holy in everything you do, just as God who chose
you is holy.
(1 Peter 1:14-15, NLT)

It was almost time for bed when my sister and I decided to relax and watch a television program we'd watched many times before. Only it turned out not to be relaxing at all. Instead, we were shocked, disgusted, and appalled when in less than four minutes the show introduced a perverse storyline, explained how this perversion took place, and began persuading the public that this clearly anti-Biblical lifestyle was normal and acceptable. (We know this much only because it was introduced so casually and quickly that it took us a minute to realize what was happening.)

As soon as we caught on, we moved on. When a little research showed that this was going to be a new plot line, we deleted the program from our DVR recording schedule. (We record everything at our house because I HATE commercials.) We will not be watching this show again because continuing watching at this point would be compromising with sin. Instead, we choose to live up to a higher standard.

A few days later, we were faced with another choice, only this time it was a fellow Christian challenging us to give up a long-held personal conviction. They argued that our commitment was illogical and old-fashioned and we needed to *"get with the times."*

Once again, we were faced with the choice to compromise our conviction and participate in an activity that was kind of tempting or choose once again to stick to our higher standard. (We chose to stick with our conviction.)

Both of these incidents made me start thinking about why we continue to choose to live by a higher standard. As I thought about why we continue to make these decisions, I have to admit it isn't just because we want to avoid the potential punishment that may come with sin. (Although that would be a good reason.) Instead, I believe that God rewards people when they choose to hold to the standards and principles in His Word. Personally, I don't want to do anything that would interfere with God's blessing, His favor, or His anointing on our lives. No compromise is worth that. None.

Much like the young Hebrews who chose to obey God's commands even when they had the opportunity and were actually commanded to disobey, we have found that when we choose to take the risk and obey God, God blesses your choice. (Daniel 1:8-21)

"But aren't you afraid you're missing out on something?"

Honestly, no.

Higher Standards

But I'll tell you one thing I absolutely do not want to miss: God's perfect will for my life and the opportunity to fully walk in my calling. Because even though society's standard, and even sometimes popular church opinion, about what may be right or wrong may change over the years, God's Word does not.

We are still called to be different.

We are still called to live for God and show the world what it means to be a Christian.

We are called to be a light in a dark place, not just blend in with the darkness hoping the world will like us and want to be with us. The call to sanctification and becoming more like Jesus is still relevant. It is still what we are called to pursue and who we are called to be.

Before we go any further, let me say this chapter is not meant to be a discussion of legalism versus grace. God's grace covers all of our sins when we repent. It is meant to be a discussion of the need to abandon compromise in our lives and live the deeper, godly life as we do whatever it takes to fulfill our God-given calling.

> **It's time we abandon both legalism as well as compromising and just live the way the Bible tells us to live.**

It's time we abandon both legalism as well as compromising and just live the way the Bible tells us to live. If we are truly going to walk in our calling, we need to live by Biblical standards.

A large part of our calling as men and women who are following God is a call to pursue godliness. It's a resounding theme throughout the New Testament, written about by Paul, Peter, John, and even

Jesus. Here are a few examples:

> *For God has not called us to live in sin. He has called us to live a holy life. (1 Thessalonians 4:7, NLV)*

> *You ought to live holy and godly lives as you look forward to the day of God and speed its coming.*
> *(2 Peter 3:11-12, NIV)*

These are just a few Scriptures that reinforce the idea that our calling is directly tied to God's desire for us to live righteous, godly lives.

But how do we make this practical?

It begins by spending time in God's presence because God is complete holiness. The more time we spend with Him in prayer, Bible reading, both private and corporate worship, speaking in tongues and just resting in His Spirit, the more we will become familiar with His pureness and desire it in our own lives. As we spend time with Him, the more we will crave His presence and be convicted by things that offend His purity.

As we spend time in God's Word learning what He sees as sin and what He sees as proper behavior for His followers, we are equipped to make better choices and develop personal godliness in our own lives.

Let's get even more practical. Throughout the rest of this chapter, we're going to talk about four specific areas where all Christians who want to walk in their calling should be pursuing becoming like God and abandoning sin. You'll notice we've been very careful to use only Scriptures from the New Testament to show that these teachings apply to all of us even as we live under grace in Christ. Remember, we are talking about living a Christ-like life that is worthy of the calling that we are privileged to have received. Let's start with the first one:

Abstaining from Sexual Sin

1 Thessalonians 4:3-7 says:

> *It is God's will that you should be sanctified: that you should avoid sexual immorality; that each of you should learn to control your own body in a way that is holy and honorable,*
>
> *not in passionate lust like the pagans, who do not know God; and that in this matter no one should wrong or take advantage of a brother or sister.*
>
> *The Lord will punish all those who commit such sins, as we told you and warned you before.*
>
> *For God did not call us to be impure, but to live a holy life.*
>
> *Therefore, anyone who rejects this instruction does not reject a human being but God, the very God who gives you his Holy Spirit. (NIV)*

Going even further Ephesians 5:3 says:

> *But among you there must not be even a hint of sexual immorality, or of any kind of impurity, or of greed, because these are improper for God's holy people. (NIV)*

Both of these verses make it clear that, as Christians, part of our God-given calling is to bring our sexual lives under the control of the Holy Spirit and flee sexual immorality.

What is sexual immorality?

Essentially, it is all forms of sex that are outside of God's original design for sexuality. God's will is that sex be exclusive to one man and one woman within a monogamous, loving, marriage relationship.

Married or single, this is God's standard. Of course, sexual immorality also includes: pornography in any form, masturbation, sexting or online sex, robot-sex, visiting ladies or gentleman's clubs and watching their entertainment or participating in the offered activities, or watching any form of sexual entertainment online. All of these things are misappropriations of God's original design, and, according to the New Testament, they are a sin.

Think this is too radical? In Matthew 5:28, Jesus says that even looking at someone lustfully is a sin. If Jesus says, that as His followers, we should seek this level of radical purity in even our thought life, then the very least we can do is seek to be accountable for our actions.

The truth is that even though we live in a society that says that sexual freedom is normal and promiscuity is no big deal, according to the Bible, sexual sin is deadly serious. Galatians 5:19-21 lists sexual immorality among the sins that will keep people out of Heaven. In God's eyes, this is not a gray area—it is a matter of obedience.

So what do you do if you find yourself trapped in any of these sins?

Follow the instructions found in 1 Corinthians 6:18 and ***"Flee from sexual immorality." (NIV)***

Start by asking God to forgive you for the sin you are committing. Then follow through in true repentance and do whatever it takes—take whatever steps are necessary. This may include ending or altering a relationship where you are not following God's plan for sexuality. Some who are living together may have to get their own apartment. It may be time to decide if you are going to get married or move on as a single person obeying the Bible.

If you're struggling with your thought life, you may consider a v-chip, internet accountability, Covenant Eyes, give up a beloved program or movie, have an accountability partner, or even go to counseling to begin living a sexually pure life.

Abstaining from Occultic Practices

Dear children, keep yourself from idols. (I John 5:21, NIV)

As Christians, most of us read this Scripture and think, *"Naturally, I don't worship idols."* And yet, there is a growing trend in Western culture to incorporate the practices of false religions such as Hinduism, Buddhism, and other Eastern religions that do practice idol worship into our daily lives. When we casually adopt an activity derived from false religions, we are opening ourselves up to the same demonic influences as if we personally went to the temple and worshiped the idols.

If we want to live a life completely devoted to God, as Christians, we need to avoid any and all practices that find their origins in these religions. This includes the popular trends toward animism, transcendental meditation, and yoga. (I almost left the yoga discussion out of the men's version of this book, but then I realized that one, some men do yoga, and two, men need to know the dangers of yoga so that they can stop their wives and daughters from doing it.) Because here is the truth: these things are not harmless; they are dangerous.

Meditation isn't just a way to relax. Yoga isn't just exercise.

I recently heard a quote that hit me as so true:

"To say the positions of yoga are no more than exercise is tantamount to saying water baptism is just aqua aerobics." [1]

The truth is that whenever we play around with the paranormal, false religions, or the occult, we are inviting demonic influences to affect our lives. Just like you wouldn't invite a pack of wolves to come into your home and ravish your family, a wise Christian will not participate in activities related to foreign religions that will invite demonic elements into your home to destroy you and your family spiritually.

This principle doesn't just apply to false religions. It applies to any form of occult practice, magic, or witchcraft. This includes Ouija boards, terra cards, palm reading, horoscopes, fortune-telling, dungeons and dragons and any other board game, video game, virtual game, or form of entertainment that has its roots in the occult. It also involves movies, television shows, and novels that are really just exhibitions of the paranormal, people interacting with demons, magic or witchcraft, or practicing the occult.

We need to realize that these things are not harmless fun. They don't fall into the category of *"gray areas"* that will not affect your soul. Instead, Galatians 5:9-10 takes them very seriously when it lists idol worship and witchcraft among the sins that will keep a person from inheriting the kingdom of God.

> *The acts of the flesh are obvious: sexual immorality, impurity and debauchery;*
>
> *idolatry and witchcraft;*
>
> *hatred, discord, jealousy, fits of rage, selfish ambition, dissensions, factions and envy; drunkenness, orgies, and the like.*
>
> *I warn you, as I did before, that those who live like this will not inherit the kingdom of God. (NIV)*

From a personal standpoint, I have seen what choosing to participate in these types of activities can cause. You see, I come from a line of ancestors who thought that playing around with false religions and the occult was no big deal. They openly embraced things like Pow-Wow-ing, astrology, horoscopes, Ouija boards, and other forms of the occult.

Only instead of being innocuous, not only they, but their children and grandchildren, suffered the consequences of their choices. As someone who has seen the heartache and pain, who has sat through the counseling sessions as my parents and I (and my sister) fought for our spiritual freedom, I can assure you that dabbling with false religions, the occult, and the paranormal are NOT worth it. When you invite demonic influences into your life, they cause destruction.

There are other ways to exercise. Other games to play, other books to read, and other movies to watch that do not involve false religions and the occult.

So please, before you jump into an activity or a movie or a game that involves magic, witchcraft, or the occult—do your research. Find out if there is even a hint of a religion other than Christianity. If there is, avoid it. It's that simple.

Choose to obey 1 John 5:21, and in every way, *"Keep yourself from idols."*

Abstaining from Alcohol and Recreational Drugs

We live in a society where alcohol is easily accessible and socially acceptable. It's seen as an ingredient for a good time. Even in Christian circles, it is becoming more and more common to condone social drinking. I know that this topic has become controversial among Christians over the last few decades. I was in college when I first heard the argument that this was a *"gray area"* that fell into Paul's teaching on freedom in Christ. So, yes, I've heard all of the pro-alcohol and pro-recreational drug arguments, including that Paul told Timothy to *"drink a little wine for your illness." (1 Timothy 5:23)*

However, this is just one side of a very weak argument. As

Christians who are committed to doing whatever it takes to live godly lives, I believe it is very important that we hear a different perspective.

Starting with the fact that there is no doubt that the New Testament clearly states that as followers of Christ, drunkenness and intoxication are regularly included among the list of sins Christians are called to avoid.

1 Peter 4:3 says:

> *You've already put in your time in that God-ignorant way of life, partying night after night, a drunken and profligate life. Now it's time to be done with it for good. (The Message)*

Romans 13:12-14 says:

> *So let us put aside the deeds of darkness and put on the armor of light.*
>
> *Let us behave decently, as in the daytime, not in carousing and drunkenness, not in sexual immorality and debauchery, not in dissension and jealousy.*
>
> *Rather, clothe yourselves with the Lord Jesus Christ, and do not think about how to gratify the desires of the flesh. (NIV)*

1 Timothy 3:3 and Titus 1:7 state that anyone who wants to be in leadership in the church should refrain from drunkenness.

But what about Timothy? Didn't Paul tell him it was alright to drink a little wine? Well, like the Assemblies of God Position Paper on Abstinence from Alcohol says, *"Paul's counsel is a recommendation for medicinal use. Timothy was probably drinking only local water or other nonalcoholic liquids (likely impure). That he needed to be encouraged to take a little wine for his stomach's sake certainly indicates that regular use of wine was not his lifestyle."* [2]

Let's be clear: We aren't talking about alcohol or drugs for medicinal use. When it comes to the topic of alcohol's role in living a holy life, we are talking about social drinking—using alcohol and drugs in a recreational setting. This has nothing to do with Paul's instructions to Timothy.

Instead, it is about choosing to compromise and participate in an activity that has traditionally been considered improper for Christians. Throughout my years of studying the Bible, I cannot find any passage of Scripture that says participating in this type of activity is a good idea. (Although many say that using alcohol is unwise.)

If you would like to read a thoroughly laid out Scriptural argument encouraging Christians to abstain from alcohol and recreational drugs, I encourage you to take a few minutes and read *the Assemblies of God Position Paper - Abstinence from Alcohol*. For the sake of this chapter, here are a few reasons that I believe that alcohol and recreational drugs are not compatible with walking in your calling.

The reality is that alcohol is not a harmless drink. It is ethanol, which is a sedative. Above the Influence says *"When alcohol is consumed, it is absorbed into a person's bloodstream. From there, it affects the central nervous system (the brain and spinal cord), which controls virtually all body functions. Alcohol actually blocks some of the messages trying to get to the brain. This alters a person's perceptions, emotions, movement, vision, and hearing. Some of the side effects of drinking can include difficulty walking, blurred vision, slurred speech, slowed reaction times, impaired memory and blackouts, mental confusion, paralysis of the nerves that move the eyes, difficulty with muscle coordination, persistent learning and memory problems, liver disease, and unintentional injuries."* [3]

This is one of my biggest objections to alcohol and recreational drugs: Why would we want to give over this kind of control to any substance? Why do we want to have our judgment impaired in this way? How can we be a good representative of Christ while we are under the influence?

Here are a few *"what if's"* to consider:

What if we say or do something that ruins our reputation, or more importantly Christ's reputation, while we are under the influence of alcohol or recreational drugs?

What if our inhibitions are so lowered that we commit a sin we would otherwise avoid?

God forbid, how will our testimony ever recover if we injure someone while driving under the influence?

These are real, practical questions that we need to evaluate and ask, *"Is it worth the risk?"*

I do not believe it is. Instead, I believe that as Christians seeking to live a holy life, we need to heed Peter's warning and choose to *"Be alert and of sober mind. Your enemy the devil prowls around like a roaring lion looking for someone to devour." (1 Peter 5:8, NIV)*

As Christians seeking to live a life worthy of our calling, I believe we need to obey the teaching of Ephesians 5:18 that says, *"Do not get drunk on wine, which leads to debauchery. Instead, be filled with the Spirit." (NIV)*

The truth in this Scripture is that alcohol is a cheap substitute for the Holy Spirit. He can fill every need that you have without alcohol. Hence, for the believer, there is no excuse for drinking.

For instance, if you feel stressed, pray and ask the Holy Spirit for help.

Do you need courage? The Holy Spirit can give you all the strength and courage that you need.

You don't need to drown your sorrows. The Bible says that God wants to heal our broken hearts.

Do you need to feel happier? The joy of the Lord is our strength.

The truth is that if you take a hard look at the practicalities, there is no benefit to alcohol and recreational drugs for a Christian. To those who still feel that these arguments are not enough and that they NEED to have the right to drink, I have to ask, *"Why is this so important to you?"*

If alcohol and recreational drugs are no big deal—-just a pleasurable gray area—-why are you willing to go to the mat for it?

Alcohol is a cheap substitute for the Holy Spirit. He can fill every need that you have without alcohol. Hence, for the believer, there is no excuse for drinking.

Why are you so aggressively willing to do whatever it takes to be able to drink instead of sacrificing this small pleasure to do whatever it takes to live a holy life and live out your calling?

A while back, there was a men's ministry leader who was constantly asking me to let him lead a workshop at a Mantour. Eventually, I had a topic I felt he would do well with, and asked him to speak. However, after he saw our speaker agreement, which includes signing an agreement saying that you do not drink alcohol, he contacted me and refused to sign. His daily glass of beer was more important to him than sharing as a speaker. As a result, he didn't get the speaker spot. My question to him is the same I bring to you today..."*Why is it so important to you?*"

If you aren't willing to sacrifice such an easy thing for God, will you make the tougher sacrifices God will inevitably ask of you?

Again, why is this so important to you?

It's something to think about. But for the sake of brevity, let's move on.

Abstinence From Ungodly Entertainment

It was late at night and Adessa and I were getting ready to watch a rerun of very popular television show when our Dad walked into the room. Knowing that he had issues with some specific sins in his past, and knowing there would be plenty of sexual innuendo in the show, we waited until he left the room to start watching. Only the Holy Spirit wasn't happy with our choice.

At that moment, He spoke to me and said, *"If it isn't okay for your dad to watch, why is it okay for you?"*

Ouch! Bullseye! That was it, we haven't watched that show again. But honestly, the real question should have been even deeper… *"If your Heavenly Father wouldn't be comfortable watching it, why are you comfortable watching it?"*

When it comes to the topic of doing whatever it takes to live godly lives, one of the biggest areas that Christians need to evaluate is our choice of entertainment. Simply put: if your choice of entertainment does not fall within the guidelines of Philippians 4:8, then you shouldn't be entertaining it.

Let's take a look at that verse:

> **Finally, brothers and sisters, whatever is true, whatever is noble, whatever is right, whatever is pure, whatever is lovely, whatever is admirable—if anything is excellent or praiseworthy—think about such things. (NIV)**

This applies to television shows, movies, music, and the things we watch online. As Christians, we need to be careful to pursue godliness in our entertainment.

"What's the big deal? It's just entertainment."

However, the truth is that entertainment influences us. It affects the way we think, act, speak, and it alters our view of God, ourselves, and the world around us. If we want to live pure lives, then we need to stay away from impure influences.

As it says in 1 Corinthians 15:33, **"Bad company corrupts good character." (NIV)**

In today's technological society, the things we watch and listen to are the company we keep.

For this reason, Adessa and I have committed to being extremely careful to pursue purity in our choice of entertainment. Toward this end, I've taken several pro-active steps:

1. I set the parental controls on the television to PG and blocked all sexual content, language, and violence.

2. I signed myself, Adessa, and my dad up to use Covenant Eyes on all of our devices and take advantage of the accountability feature so that someone else is made aware of everything we see.

3. We do not go to movie theaters and are extremely selective about the movies we watch on television. (Again, we take advantage of the parental filter.)

4. We are extremely careful in our choice of music avoiding anything with profanity, sexual content, or foul language.

I've taken these steps because I truly believe that godliness is still relevant. It is still what we are called to pursue and who we are called to be.

This brings us to this chapter's radical challenge:

Spend some time with the Holy Spirit answering these questions:

"Are there any areas of my life where I need to do a better job of pursuing godliness?"

"Am I compromising and making excuses rather than obeying God's Word?"

Dare to be hard on yourself. Ask:

"Why am I embracing the culture instead of God's ways?"

"Who is influencing my choices and are they a good influence?"

"Is the excuse, 'Well, everybody else is doing it' really a valid argument?"

"Are there areas where I need to reevaluate and perhaps abandon my choices?"

"If I stay on my current path, what sin will I be tolerating 15 years from now?"

I challenge you to spend some time with the Holy Spirit genuinely answering these questions and then allow His influence to affect your future choices and behavior.

Choose to accept God's call to live a life worthy of your calling in every area of your life.

Become the person God wants you to be so that you can do what He has called you to do.

Group Study Questions:

1. Why is godly living so important for a believer?

2. This chapter stated, *"It's time we abandon both legalism as well as compromising and just live the way the Bible tells us to live."* What does this mean?

3. What are some of the influences in your life that need to be abandoned if you want to live a godly life?

4. Are there any areas of your life where you need to do a better job of pursuing purity and godliness?

5. Are you compromising and making excuses rather than obeying God's Word?

6. After reading this chapter, what is one thing you will put into practice or one thing you will change in your life?

7. How can we as a group help you do this?

Radical Challenge:

Spend some time with the Holy Spirit answering these questions:

"Are there any areas of my life where I need to do a better job of pursuing purity and godliness?"

"Am I compromising and making excuses rather than obeying God's Word?"

Dare to be hard on yourself. Ask:

"Why am I embracing the culture instead of God's ways?"

"Who is influencing my choices and are they a good influence?"

"Is the excuse, 'Well, everybody else is doing it' really a valid argument?"

"Are there areas where I need to reevaluate and perhaps abandon my choices?"

"If I stay on my current path, what sin will I be tolerating 15 years from now?"

Finally, make the lifestyle changes necessary to do whatever it takes to pursue godliness and live a life worthy of your calling.

Chapter Ten

Honesty Really Is The Best Policy

*Joyful are people of integrity,
who follow the instructions of the Lord.
(Psalm 119:1, NLT)*

"*Son, one thing I've learned over my lifetime is that there's never a need to lie.*"

I was in my early twenties when a garage door salesman sat at our dining room table and spoke these words. It was the first time we were involved in making a really big household purchase. Having just been through a time when we were lied to and cheated, Adessa and I were skeptical of everything and everyone. Trying to make sure we were making the right choice and that we weren't being cheated again, we peppered the poor guy with questions. To be honest, we were a little rude in our zealousness.

Rather than being offended, he spoke these words that I'll never forget as he stood behind his product and his integrity. (By the way, the door was still in great shape after twenty years when we took it down to convert our garage to an office. Today, it's hanging in a friend's garage.)

Since that day, I've thought about this man over and over again as I've seen the importance of everyday integrity… *"There is never a need to lie."* Over time, I've learned that personal integrity is an integral part of living a life worthy of your calling. Unfortunately, I've seen people who had all the ability, talent, education, and personality in the world lose everything because they didn't have personal integrity. On the other hand, I've seen people who didn't have the same stellar credentials thrive because people were drawn to their character and integrity. It really is a make or break issue.

> **Personal integrity is an integral part of living a life worthy of your calling.**

I know that in our ministry, it is one of the first things we look for when we are partnering with someone. Whether it be a speaker, someone to do a job, or a volunteer, integrity is at the top of our list. Although we will tolerate a lot with understanding, if we find you are lying to us, we won't continue the partnership. You just cannot trust someone who doesn't value the truth. We are not the only people with this policy. That's just one of the reasons that personal integrity needs to be a top priority in the life of every Christian.

One of the first areas where we need to be people of integrity is:

Being Honest About Ourselves.

Essentially, don't misrepresent yourself.

I remember listening to someone responsible for hiring workers

Honesty Really Is The Best Policy

for an annual event share how difficult it was to be constantly bombarded by people who wanted to work for them. This person said that one of the most annoying things was how people misrepresented themselves. They'd say *"international speaker"* only to find that this meant they went on a missions trip to Mexico with their youth group. Some would make it appear they'd graduated from colleges they only briefly attended. They'd list skills they didn't possess. Some people even sent photos from ten to fifteen years ago hoping no one would notice they'd aged and didn't look the same. Honestly, some of the stories this person shared were funny, while others made you say, *"What were they thinking?"* Still, they all had one thing in common: resumes with misrepresentations were thrown away.

This person was sharing these stories with a group of people, including some who were just starting their careers, to make the point: Don't follow this pattern.

Don't lie about who you are to boost your reputation, because in the end it destroys your reputation.

Instead, be yourself. Be genuine. Be authentic. Just as He did with the twelve disciples, the Holy Spirit can empower you and anoint you despite your inadequacies. However, He will not and cannot be part of a deception. So don't sabotage yourself by putting on airs, padding your resume (or your social media profile) with lies, or misrepresenting yourself. Instead, be a person of integrity. Present yourself as you are and give the Holy Spirit room to work in your favor. Next,

Be honest in your business and financial dealings.

I cannot overemphasize the importance of this point. We need to understand that people take issues regarding their money very personally. When you misrepresent yourself financially, fail to pay back a loan, leave someone holding the bag financially, or steal from them, it isn't just a financial loss, but it feels like a betrayal. They trusted you, and you violated that trust. In many cases, it marks you for life as a person who cannot be trusted.

I remember an instance where we went into a business deal with someone who had a lack of financial integrity. Even though contracts were signed, they did not stick to the terms and we were left paying off the incurred expenses while they walked away from the deal. Financially, it was difficult; but the sadder part was the broken relationship. How could someone we trusted cause us this much pain? Years and years later, the bills are paid and the financial issue is resolved. We have chosen to forgive them, but honestly, we will never trust them again. Also, it's made us extremely cautious about going into future business dealings. We've learned that personal integrity is a priority above all else when it comes to finances.

So how can this be practically applied?

Don't misrepresent yourself on financial applications or loan papers.

Be honest with yourself about your personal finances, create a budget, and live within your means.

Don't take out loans for things you can't afford, and if you borrow money, pay it back, even if it was from the government. If you borrowed money from a person or a bank, go to them and work out a plan to pay it back. Honor your financial responsibilities.

Don't cheat on your taxes and completely pay your tithe. Remember, integrity also applies to things belonging to God.

Don't steal just because you think a company can afford it.

If you are an employer, pay your employees well. Do a good job for the people who hire you. Offer a good product at a fair price. If you are an employee, give your employer an honest day's work. Show up on time. Work hard. Don't take advantage of them.

Honor God in every way with your money and be completely above board in all areas of your finances. Remember that it isn't just about dollars and cents—it's about integrity.

The same principles apply when it comes to the area of commitment.

This one falls into two parts: First, don't make any commitments unless you fully intend to keep them. Second, if you make a commitment, do everything in your power to honor your word.

> First, don't make any commitments unless you are really committed to keeping them. Second, if you've made a commitment, do everything in your power to honor your word.

Please, let me say that I understand that there are times when emergency circumstances or unforeseen illness prevent us from keeping our commitments. This happens to all of us and is unavoidable. In situations like this, an apology and explanation will usually cause most people to be understanding and realize life happens. These situations have nothing to do with integrity.

Instead, I'm talking about people who have a reputation for not keeping their commitments. We've all met them. The person who always RSVPs, but never shows up. The guy who is first to volunteer, but never makes it to the event.

To them, unreliability has become a bad habit. They remind you of Scriptures like Proverbs 25:19 which say:

> *Like a broken tooth or a lame foot is reliance on the*

> *unfaithful in a time of trouble.* (NIV)

> *Like billowing clouds that bring no rain is the person who talks big but never produces. (Proverbs 25:14, The Message)*

For instance, I know a man who has a reputation for always being the first person to volunteer to make a donation whenever a need is presented. He stands up in front of the crowd and makes a big show of the donation he's promising to make. Unfortunately, over time, he's also developed a bad reputation. Behind the scenes, people tell each other, *"Don't count on that promise. He usually doesn't follow through."* It's become his reputation.

When it comes down to it, our reputation is one of the most important ways that our integrity affects our calling. Because your actions, not your words, create your reputation. Your reputation opens or closes doors of opportunity for you to walk in your calling.

That's why it's essential that you develop a reputation for being reliable and trustworthy if you want to fully walk in your calling. This comes by being a person who keeps their commitments even when it's inconvenient. If you aren't good at keeping commitments, then don't make them.

Don't accept the public praise for things you know you can't privately do.

Instead, take a moment and evaluate whether you can keep your commitment. Be honest with others and yourself about what you can and will do. Although it seems like this will make people like you less, they will actually trust you more because they will respect your honesty and integrity.

As Proverbs 25:13 says, ***"Reliable friends who do what they say are like cool drinks in sweltering heat—refreshing!"*** *(The Message).*

As I am writing this, we are in a 100-degree heatwave, so I get how refreshing cool water can be. Being reliable is the same refreshing experience for those who encounter us.

Speaking of reputation, there is another area of integrity that I think we need to discuss:

The necessity of having integrity in our relationships with the opposite sex.

In a previous chapter, we talked about the need to pursue holiness in our sexual life. However, in the context of reputation and integrity, I think we need to go a step further and *"Abstain from all appearance of evil." (1 Thessalonians 5:22, KJV)*

Lately, it's become popular to mock what is referred to as the Billy Graham rule: a personal conviction held by Billy Graham that he would not be alone with a woman, even in an elevator.

Honestly, I get it, in modern society it seems old-fashioned. Yet, I've seen too many people who thought they would never need this rule because they would never fall into temptation end up destroying their lives, their families, their reputations, and sometimes their careers. I'm starting to think it's wise advice. After hearing stories from people who did nothing wrong but were falsely accused by people who wanted to hurt them, I'm convinced that this rule is essential to our integrity.

It isn't, as the critics suggest, an insult to the other person. The Bible tells us that we are to see members of the opposite sex who are not our significant other as our brothers and sisters. (I Timothy 5:1-2) Wouldn't we want to do all we could to protect not just ourselves, but also our brother or sisters?

Honestly, what's the big deal about meeting in public, leaving a door open, cc'ing someone on an email, or doing whatever it takes to maintain your integrity?

In the end, that's what it's all about—doing whatever it takes to maintain your integrity in every area of your life. Whether it involves your personal life, your financial life, or how you keep your commitments, as the garage door repairman says, *"There's never a good reason to lie."* Instead, there is always wisdom in choosing to be a person of integrity.

So here's this chapter's radical challenge: Take some time and evaluate yourself in all four of these areas.

In which area do you struggle most? Where do you need to improve?

What practical steps can you take to improve so that you will have a reputation as a person of integrity?

After you've answered these questions, determine that you will do whatever it takes to change your reputation so that you will be a person of integrity. Don't let a lack of integrity deter your calling. Instead, do whatever it takes to protect yourself, your reputation and your calling.

Group Study Questions:

1. How does integrity work with walking in your calling?

2. How do you demonstrate integrity in your finances? What steps can you take to have even more financial integrity?

3. Why is it important to always keep your commitments?

4. Why is it important to be a person of integrity as you interact with the opposite sex?

5. What practical steps do you need to implement in your interactions?

6. In what area of your life do you struggle the most to be a person of integrity? What practical steps can you take to improve?

7. After reading this chapter, what is one thing you will put into practice or one thing you will change in your life?

8. How can we as a group help you do this?

Radical Challenge:

Take some time and evaluate yourself in all four of these areas.

Ask yourself: In which area do I struggle most? Where do I need to improve?

Take it a step further and ask the most honest person in your life if they see any areas in your life that lack integrity.

Now look at your weakest area and write down three practical steps that you can take to begin walking in personal integrity. Then start doing whatever it takes to change your reputation.

Chapter Eleven

Love Really Is A Verb

*No matter what I say, what I believe, and what I do,
I'm bankrupt without love.
(I Corinthians 13:3, The Message)*

I love reading the stories in the New Testament when Jesus would confront the establishment swamp rats in Jerusalem. They would come at Him, intent on making Him look bad or embarrassing Him. Their goal was to discredit Him and show everyone that He wasn't as qualified to be a spiritual leader as they were.

Let's look at one of these situations.

> *Later they sent some of the Pharisees and Herodians to Jesus to catch him in his words. They came to him and said, "Teacher, we know that you are a man of integrity. You aren't swayed by others, because you pay no attention to who they are; but you teach the way of God in accordance with the truth. Is it right to pay the imperial tax to Caesar*

> *or not? Should we pay or shouldn't we?"*
>
> *But Jesus knew their hypocrisy. "Why are you trying to trap me?" he asked. "Bring me a denarius and let me look at it." They brought the coin, and he asked them, "Whose image is this? And whose inscription?"*
>
> *"Caesar's," they replied.*
>
> *Then Jesus said to them, "Give back to Caesar what is Caesar's and to God what is God's." (Mark 12:13-17, NIV)*

This was meant to be the ultimate *"gotcha"* moment.

Determined to trip Him up, they peppered Jesus with impossible questions hoping He'd either break Jewish law, Roman law, or at least seriously offend the sensibilities of the crowds who hung on every word that He said.

Yet, despite their best efforts, their plans failed as Jesus answered every question perfectly. That's when an honest man sincerely asked a question.

> *One of the teachers of the law came and heard them debating. Noticing that Jesus had given them a good answer, he asked him,*
>
> *"Of all the commandments, which is the most important?"*
>
> *"The most important one," answered Jesus, "is this: 'Hear, O Israel: The Lord our God, the Lord is one.*
>
> *Love the Lord your God with all your heart and with all your soul and with all your mind and with all your strength.'*
>
> *The second is this: 'Love your neighbor as yourself.'*

There is no commandment greater than these."
(Mark 12:28-31, NIV)

With that answer, Jesus explained how the character trait of love combined with love as an action ties into the concept of doing whatever it takes to live a life worthy of your calling. As the religious leader went on to reply,

> *The religion scholar said,*
>
> *"A wonderful answer, Teacher! So lucid and accurate—that God is one and there is no other.*
>
> *And loving him with all passion and intelligence and energy, and loving others as well as you love yourself.*
>
> *Why, that's better than all offerings and sacrifices put together!"*
>
> *(Mark 12:32-33, The Message)*

That's what it means to truly take on the challenge to do whatever it takes to follow God—to love Him with of all of your passion, all of your intelligence, and all of your energy. Giving every single part of your life for Him, simply because you love Him.

Because here's the truth: dedication to an idea or a desire to advance yourself will only sustain you for so long. As we see with men like Judas, these motivations may cause you to begin following Jesus, but they won't convince you to keep following Him when times are difficult. When God calls you to walk down a path you wouldn't have chosen, when obeying God demands sacrifice and obedience, when God's ways are different than your ways, and especially when persecution comes, these motivations will become your stumbling block. In these circumstances, only a passionate, committed love for God will help you say, *"No matter what, I am all in. I committed to following God, and I'm not changing my mind. Even if I have to lose everything for God, I will still follow Him because I love Him."*

This level of commitment is only fueled by love. It's the first part of the greatest commandment.

Then comes the second half of the greatest commandment: loving your neighbor as yourself. Granted, this one is a little more difficult.

Because of its difficulty, many ask, *"Who is my neighbor?"* Here's how Jesus answered that question when it was presented to Him:

> *Jesus replied with a story:*
>
> *"A Jewish man was traveling from Jerusalem down to Jericho, and he was attacked by bandits. They stripped him of his clothes, beat him up, and left him half dead beside the road.*
>
> *By chance a priest came along. But when he saw the man lying there, he crossed to the other side of the road and passed him by. A Temple assistant walked over and looked at him lying there, but he also passed by on the other side.*
>
> *Then a despised Samaritan came along, and when he saw the man, he felt compassion for him. Going over to him, the Samaritan soothed his wounds with olive oil and wine and bandaged them. Then he put the man on his own donkey and took him to an inn, where he took care of him. The next day he handed the innkeeper two silver coins, telling him, 'Take care of this man. If his bill runs higher*

than this, I'll pay you the next time I'm here.'

Now which of these three would you say was a neighbor to the man who was attacked by bandits?" Jesus asked.

The man replied, "The one who showed him mercy." Then Jesus said, "Yes, now go and do the same." (Luke 10:30-37, NLT)

In the context of this parable, we see Jesus define *"your neighbor"* as anyone that you come in contact with during your daily life—anyone in your sphere of influence. This begins with the inner circle of your immediate family and moves out to your extended family. It includes the people who live near you, who work near you, the people you carpool with to work or school, your friends and your enemies, the other parents at your children's school or on their sports team, the woman at the grocery store, the guy at the restaurant. Basically, anyone that you encounter during your day is your neighbor and you are responsible to show love to them.

> **Do what Jesus said and treat people the way that you would want to be treated.**

But how can you show love to that many people?

Start by doing what Jesus said and treating people the way that you would want to be treated.

Take this parable for example. In this story, the man had an obvious need. He'd just experienced a crisis—he'd been beaten, stripped of everything, including his clothes, and left by the side of the road for dead. At that moment, he needed safety and medical help. In today's terms, he needed someone to call 911. He needed urgent, practical care.

Yet, the first two people who walked by did nothing. They just ignored the situation and went on with their own lives. It was only the good Samaritan who stopped, went out of his way, and showed the man love by meeting his practical needs.

As followers of God, we need to realize that part of our calling is to follow the example of the good Samaritan and to show love to people by meeting their practical needs. When we encounter someone who has an obvious need, we should do all that we can to meet it.

Part of this involves being involved in community outreaches that meet the needs of those who are in desperate situations. As Christians, we need to be donating both our time and our finances so that people can see the love of God practically demonstrated to the most hurting and helpless among us.

And yet, as important as charity work is, I don't believe it totally encompasses our call to meet the practical needs of those around us. Instead, I believe that as Christians we also need to be aware of the practical needs of the people around us and find a way to demonstrate God's love to them by meeting their needs.

For instance, does someone need a ride to the hospital or someone to be with them as support through a difficult doctor's appointment?

Would a family appreciate a home-cooked meal during a time of crisis or grief?

Could you cut the grass for the elderly woman across the street who is struggling with pain?

Does a young couple need a few hours to themselves, but can't afford a baby sitter?

Does a young man without a father need a mentor who is willing to shoot hoops and just listen?

Ultimately, when the Holy Spirit points someone out that has an obvious need or allows someone to cross your path who needs help, how do you respond?

Do you understand, that as a Christian, you are called to show love by helping to meet that need no matter what it costs you personally?

Are you willing to do whatever it takes to answer that call?

These are hard questions, but they are questions that I truly believe we all need to ask ourselves from time to time. Because it is just so easy to fall into the trap of minding your own business. (Really, that's what the priest and the Temple assistant did—they kept walking and stayed out of it while someone's real need went unmet.) It's easy to get so busy, so wrapped up in ourselves and our problems, that we forget that the central part of our calling is to love others and show them God's love.

From time to time even the most well-meaning Christians need to ask themselves, *"Am I listening to the voice of the Holy Spirit when He shows me a practical need that I can meet? Am I responding in obedience? How can I do better?"*

Sometimes, meeting someone's practical needs is as simple as simply being nice.

Some people just need someone to listen to them.

Others just need a word of encouragement, a smile, a *"thank you so much"* to help them get through a difficult day.

Sometimes an expression of love can be as basic as just being kind.

1 Corinthians 13:4 says, **"Love is patient, love is kind." (NIV)**

Are you patient? Are you kind?

What about when the line at the grocery store is long and the clerk just made another mistake and has to take time to fix it?

Are you kind when it was your turn and someone jumped in front of you?

What about at work? Are you kind to your co-workers or do you treat them badly, take advantage of them, or use them to advance yourself?

Are the words you speak to people kind?

What about the words you speak about people? Are you gossipy, critical, or cruel, or do you use your words to lift people up and encourage them?

The truth is that love really is found in the little things. As it says in 1 Corinthians 13, we can do all of the religious, spiritual stuff right, but if we don't have love, it doesn't mean a thing.

> *If I speak with human eloquence and angelic ecstasy but don't love, I'm nothing but the creaking of a rusty gate.*
>
> *If I speak God's Word with power, revealing all his mysteries and making everything plain as day, and if I have faith that says to a mountain, "Jump," and it jumps, but I don't love, I'm nothing.*
>
> *If I give everything I own to the poor and even go to the stake to be burned as a martyr, but I don't love, I've gotten nowhere.*
>
> *So, no matter what I say, what I believe, and what I do, I'm bankrupt without love.*
> *(I Corinthians 13:1-3, The Message)*

I remember being in my early twenties when the Holy Spirit started driving this point home to me. The source He used was a little odd—a popular television show about a minister and his family. (Hey, God talks to all of us differently.) As I was watching the show, the Holy Spirit began pointing out to me how this man interacted with the people in his community.

I noticed how he and his wife always spoke kindly to people. They were friendly. They initiated conversations with everyone they came into contact with throughout their day. When someone needed to talk, they listened.

They helped the people in their community whether they attended their church or not. They were genuinely nice. People trusted them. They curbed their personal frustrations at the front door—they didn't take them out on other people.

They weren't necessarily preachy, yet they stood out in a crowd because they treated people differently than people were accustomed to being treated. They offered people hope—a way out of a difficult situation, instead of judgment and criticism. Like the good Samaritan, they met the needs of people they encountered and treated them the way they would like to be treated.

As I watched this show, the Holy Spirit spoke to my heart and said, *"Do you believe that there is a calling on your life? Then start walking in your calling today and train yourself to treat people the way they do."* That was a life-changing moment for me as I realized that I had a personal responsibility to be a representative of God to every person that I came into contact with throughout my day.

From that day forward, I began training myself to be kind. Honestly, it didn't come easy. We all have days when life is hard and we just want to growl at everyone around us. Considering this *"training"* started at a time in life when I was feeling sorry for myself, it took a lot of work. Yet, as I obeyed God and chose to *"put on"* kindness, friendliness, patience, and love, I began to see not only myself, but the people around me change.

Over the years, Adessa and I have done our best to continually live this way—showing people the love of God by simply being nice.

We go out of our way to make conversations with people.

We try to encourage people whenever possible. For instance, if we are in a long line and people are starting to turn nasty, we make sure to thank the person who is working for their time and let them know they are doing a great job. For instance, just a few days ago we were waiting for an appointment. It was impossible to miss the gentleman in front of us accusing the woman behind the counter of being a crook. Everyone heard him say, *"You're all just a bunch of thieves"* over and over again.

Granted, I have no idea what his dispute involved. However, I'm absolutely sure that the woman who was waiting on him was not responsible and was doing all she could to help him. So when it was our turn, I apologized to her on behalf of the man. I said, *"I'm sorry you were treated that way."* Then we did all we could to be as encouraging and cooperative as possible while we had our issue addressed.

I remember a time where I was driving to Delaware. I honestly don't remember if it was a Mantour, a speaking engagement, or a trip to the beach. But I remember that the line to pay my turnpike toll was taking a little long. (I need to get an EZPass!) As I finally approached the booth, I noticed that the car in front of me had four men in it, and all four of them were screaming at the toll booth worker, swearing at her, and using all of the four-letter words they could remember to berate her. It made me angry at how they were treating her, but even more, I felt so bad for this woman who was just trying to do her job to provide her income.

When it was our time to pay our toll, I said to the woman, *"Those men had no right to treat you that way, and they will never apologize for it, so allow me to apologize for them. I am so sorry they treated you that way, they were wrong, and you didn't deserve it."*

The woman was visibly surprised, but she was also touched, and you could see her relax. The tenseness in her body relaxed knowing we were not going to yell at her for the long line, and she was able to move past their behavior and go on with her day.

Of course, we don't just make it a point to encourage people after others have lost their temper. We are also very mindful that we don't allow our anger or frustration to explode on other people when we are confronted with difficult situations or inconveniences. For instance, as traveling ministers, we often run into problems with hotel rooms. Rooms we request aren't reserved, sometimes the rooms we get are dirty and need attention, other times things break and we need to completely move to other rooms. (Truly, traveling is not as glamorous as it seems.) When these things happen, we try to put the person helping us at ease, to let them know we all make mistakes. We show that we aren't angry, we just need something fixed.

As we've lived our lives this way, it's been amazing what God has been able to do. I think one of my favorite stories involves a gas station attendant who started as a stranger. Every time I would pay for my gas, I made it a point to ask her how she was doing, to have some small talk with her, and to always say, *"Have a great day!"*

Over time, as I was friendly and talked to her every time we filled up our tank, she began to see us as friends. After a while, when she saw us coming, she'd talk with me and then leave the payment room and come over to the car to chat with Adessa, too. Eventually, we were able to share with her about God, tell her about a local church she might enjoy, and even give her a copy of one of Adessa's books about finding significance in Jesus. Yet, honestly, we never set out to witness to her. We were continuing in the habit of treating people the way God would treat them, and she responded to the love she was shown.

> **Like a light in the darkness, treating people with respect and showing them love helps people identify Christians as different.**

That's one of the reasons that this character trait is such an important responsibility and such a vital part of fulfilling our calling: because we live in a world that is starving for love. They've had their fill of sensuality and romance, but they are starving for genuine human connection. Most people are almost caught off guard when someone is nice, kind, patient, and understanding. They are actually surprised! It stands out, and they remember you.

Like a light in the darkness, treating people with respect and showing them love helps people identify Christians as different. This difference allows us the opportunity to answer the question, *"Why makes you different?"* with *"I've experienced the love of God, can I tell you about Him?"*

John 13:34-35 says, ***"Let me give you a new command: Love one another. In the same way I loved you, you love one another. This is how everyone will recognize that you are my disciples—when they see the love you have for each other." (The Message)***

Today, the radical challenge I have for you is this: Can people tell you are a follower of Christ by the way you treat them?

Are you actively treating people with love?

Are you going out of your way to meet the practical needs of people?

When people are in crisis, do they know they can count on you?

Are you willing to walk across the street to listen, to be a shoulder to cry on, to take a casserole to a family in trauma, or even just have a friendly conversation?

The sad thing is that some Christians would rather travel across the globe to tell a stranger about Jesus than smile at their neighbor across the street. This isn't how it should be. We need to be the person who does what's right, who meets the need, who makes the phone call to say, *"We're here. How can I help?"*

What about inside of your church? Do you prefer to hang with your few friends in your little clique or do you welcome the stranger, the family that's obviously never been to church, the unpopular, the difficult, the person no one wants to include in their gathering?

I wonder if Paul wouldn't say to us today: **"You can have the most professional-sounding worship, the best coffee, the greatest sermons, and the most awesome light show in town…but if your church doesn't have love, it doesn't have anything."**

All of us from time to time need to check our hearts and ask, *"What can I do to make my church a more loving place?"* Then do our part to demonstrate the love of God.

Of course, what really matters is what happens outside of the church. How do we interact with people each day?

How do we speak to them? How do we treat others? Are we obsessed with ourselves and our schedule or do we go out of our way to demonstrate God's love to everyone we meet?

Here's one: How about on social media? Let me be bold here and say that I have seen too many Christians post some harsh, mean, borderline-racist words in political opposition to those trapped in the sin of homosexuality or undocumented immigrants or the political party with whom they disagree. Now, I believe Christians need to stand up for what they believe, but we cross the line when our posts are vulgar, racist, or unnecessarily cruel.

Jesus always stood for truth. He was NEVER racist or cruel about it. He ALWAYS loved the lost and used this love to push them towards the truth. Jesus NEVER condoned their sin, but He ALWAYS treated them with dignity and respect, showing them godly love. Why would anyone want to come to Jesus and enter our churches if they truly believe Christians hate them? I'm not saying compromise. I'm saying make posts that draw people to Jesus, rather than send them running from Him.

Ultimately, we all need to ask ourselves, *"What can I do to better demonstrate the love of God in my life?"*

We need to recognize that this is our calling and then begin doing whatever it takes to start actively demonstrating love to our family, to our friends, to our neighbors, and our world.

We need to recognize that our calling is to follow the greatest commandment: Love God and love others. Whatever it takes, this needs to be our mission.

Group Study Questions:

1. How does walking in our calling require genuine love of God?

2. What are the specific actions you can start taking to show love to those around you?

3. Are you willing to show love by meeting the needs of others no matter what it costs you personally?

4. Are you listening to the voice of the Holy Spirit when He shows you a practical need that you can meet? Are you responding in obedience? How can you do better?"

5. What can you do to better demonstrate the love of God in your life?

6. After reading this chapter, what is one thing you will put into practice or one thing you will change in your life?

7. How can we as a group help you do this?

Radical Challenge:

Take a moment and list the people in your sphere of influence. Start with the inner circle of your immediate family and move out including the people who live near you, who work near you, the people you carpool with to work or school, your friends and your enemies, the other parents at your children's school or on their sports team, the woman at the grocery store, the guy at the restaurant.

Ask the Holy Spirit to show you three practical ways that you can demonstrate love to the people in your life in the next week. What habits, attitudes, or actions would He like you to change?

Finally, determine to begin making these practical changes and doing whatever it takes to fulfill your calling by walking in love.

Chapter Twelve

Defeat Is NOT An Option!

I have fought the good fight,
I have finished the race,
I have kept the faith.
Now there is in store for me the crown of righteousness, which the Lord, the righteous Judge, will award to me on that day—and not only to me, but also to all who have longed for his appearing.
(2 Timothy 4:7-8, NIV)

Most of us have heard the expression, *"When the going gets tough, the tough get going."*

But what exactly is it that makes the tough get going? What is the determining factor? What's their motivation?

What keeps you going when you want to quit?

When the obstacles are bigger than you believe you can climb, when it seems impossible to complete the task in front of you, when your resources don't even come close to meeting the need, what makes you decide to take one more step forward?

What motivated Noah to build the ark when he had never even seen rain? (Genesis 6-8)

What caused Daniel to stay faithful in prayer even at the risk of his own life? (Daniel 6)

What made Shadrach, Meshach, and Abednego refuse to bow to the king's statue despite the fiery furnace? (Daniel 3)

What caused Paul to endure persecution, imprisonment, beatings, and the threat of death for no other crime than preaching the Gospel? (2 Corinthians 11:21-27)

> **Conviction. The deep, unshakeable believe that convinces you that what you are doing is God's will for your life combined with the deep unshakeable belief that the center of God's will is the only place you want to be.**

What made Peter say, *"We have to obey God rather than men?" (Acts 4:19)*

The answer is conviction. The deep, unshakeable belief that convinces you that what you are doing is God's will for your life combined with the deep unshakeable belief that the center of God's will is the only place you want to be.

Conviction is what keeps you going in the hard times.

When money is short, when the hours are long, when the struggle is real, and temptation has never been more tempting…that's when your conviction that you love God and want His perfect will for your life enables you to put one foot in front of the other and keep going.

This level of conviction is an absolute necessity when it comes to living a life worthy of your calling. It's what gives you the fire in your belly to do whatever it takes through the hard times.

Trust me when I say, everyone goes through hard times. On the days when you want to throw up your hands and say *"Enough,"* your conviction that you are following God, that you are committed to His will, and your belief that He has a purpose and a plan, will help you keep moving forward.

Here are three circumstances where this type of conviction can play a vital role in your life. First:

When You or Others Are Questioning Your Calling.

We spoke in previous chapters about the fact that there will be times when other people may not understand what God is calling you to do or they just may not agree with it. Conviction is what helps us keep going even when other people are critical of our choices. When we really believe we are walking in God's calling, other people's opinions don't matter. We've already given our lives to God…now His is the only opinion that carries weight.

For example, you and your wife may want to send your kids to a Christian school and others may criticize you for it.

You may decide to not accept a promotion that requires you to spend more time away from your family, and your co-workers may say you are insane.

God may call you to move away and take a job and your extended family may think it's unwise.

These are just several examples from a million possibilities where someone may think they know better than you about what is God's will for your life.

What do you do with the words of these well-meaning people? More importantly, what do you do when their words begin to cast doubts and fears in your mind?

That's when your conviction that you've sought God's will, you prayed, you have confirmation from Him, and you believe you are following His will, gives you the courage and fortitude to hold your ground and continue on God's path for your life.

I remember a time many years ago when God's plan for my life didn't make a lot of sense. Even though I truly believed I was following God's plan for my life, I had very little to offer as proof to anyone looking in from the outside that it was God's will that I spend my days being a support system for my Mom as our family walked through an extremely difficult time.

One day I remember a very well-meaning friend telling us, *"You guys need to make some changes. You can't keep living this way. A miracle isn't coming and you need to move from where you are and start making a different life for yourselves."*

Honestly, I know this person meant well. From a purely human perspective, it was good advice. And yet, deep down inside, I knew that God had called me to live the life I was living at the time.

In the days that followed, I genuinely checked my heart and asked, *"Is my friend right?"* The more I prayed, the more I was convinced of God's calling on my life, and I knew that I had to stay where God put me. I remembered my call to ministry and it broke my heart to think that I had to walk away from it and pursue another life. The more I prayed and sought God's heart, the more I was convinced that He wanted me serving my family right where I was. I was fully convinced that this was His will and I didn't want anything else but God's will for my life.

Looking back, I can see that it was conviction that helped me continue in a very difficult situation believing it was God's will. The funny thing is that years later after seeing God work miracles, my friend will say, *"I never thought things would turn out the way they did. It's amazing what God has done."* However, decades ago, it took conviction to thank my friend for the advice, but choose to follow God.

Of course, conviction doesn't always say *"stay"*. Often it convinces you to *"go"*—to take a leap of faith—to try something that scares you to death.

For instance, even while we are writing this book, Adessa and I are embarking on a building project that absolutely overwhelms us. We are converting our existing garage into dedicated office space for 4One Ministries. I can hear them hammering as I type. Honestly, I can't tell you how many times during this project we have said to each other at various times, *"If I didn't believe this was God's will, I'd call it off. If we didn't have concrete confirmations that God wants this to happen, it wouldn't. It cost too much, it's too hard, and it makes too many changes. Still, I know beyond a shadow of a doubt that God wants this room, so we are going forward."*

Again, conviction plays a part. Even though it scares us, even though it requires huge sacrifices and lots of people have said, *"You're going to regret giving up your garage"* we are going forward because we are convinced it is God's will. If it's His will, we'll do whatever it takes.

The second way that conviction plays a role in living a life worthy of your calling is that:

Conviction Keeps Us From Sin.

Because let's be honest: there are days when the temptation to sin is very appealing. (That's why it's called *"temptation."*) We all have moments of weakness where we wonder, *"What's the big deal?"*, *"Don't I deserve a little fun?"*, *"Will it really make that big of an impact on my life?"*, or the famous *"Everyone else is doing it."*

In those moments, the conviction that following God is worth doing whatever it takes is what keeps us on the strait and narrow choosing not to engage in sin even for a moment.

> **The conviction that following God is worth doing whatever it takes is what keeps us on the strait and narrow choosing not to engage in sin even for a moment.**

It's our conviction that God's Word is true, that obeying His Word is the best path for our lives, and that He will reward those who follow His commands, that enables us to make the choice to walk away from temptation, to do the right thing even when it hurts, and faithfully follow God's commands.

Conviction will help you stand up to even Christians who will try to pull you into their level of compromise. Conviction gives you the strength to say, *"I'm sorry, I just can't go against what I believe to be God's commands."*

Finally:

Conviction Propels Us to Keep Going When Your Calling Isn't What You Expected.

Trust me, no matter what your dream life looks like, actually walking in your calling is very different then you imagined. Real life always carries more unexpected responsibilities, obstacles, and sacrifices than we anticipate. Every calling has days that are mundane and boring, when the work is tedious or just plain messy. Sorry to disappoint, but real life can never live up to the fantasy.

For instance, I had lots of grand ideas about what it would look like to be a traveling minister. What I never imagined was carrying luggage, all of the driving, less than stellar hotel rooms, or the absolute hardest part: hitting the road when you are sick or in pain. For instance, last year during Mantour season, Adessa had a tooth pulled on Thursday and we left for a conference on Friday while she was still having an allergic reaction to the novocaine.

What kept her going among the pain and nausea and crying in the Burger King bathroom?

Conviction. Knowing that God had called us to do the conferences and it was our responsibility to do whatever it takes to obey.

The truth is that when it comes to the topic of doing *"Whatever it takes"* conviction is always going to play a leading role. It goes hand in hand with passion.

Conviction convinces us that the path we are on is God's will, and because we are passionate about following God, we keep going forward.

Conviction is what motivates us to be consistent in our time of prayer and Bible reading, believing that God is listening and has something to say to us.

It's what makes us pursue the empowerment of the Holy Spirit because we are convinced that we cannot complete the plan God has for our lives on our own.

Conviction motivates us to sacrifice and make the investments necessary to fulfill our calling believing that the sacrifices we make will produce dividends for the kingdom of God.

Conviction helps us step out in faith following God wherever He leads.

It challenges us to be humble and seek the advice of a mentor believing that their experience can be the platform we build on as we follow God's call for our lives.

The conviction that it is our responsibility to fulfill the Great Commission and help people find a personal relationship with God leads us to do whatever it takes to live a life of love.

As we said before, the conviction that God's ways are the best way to live our lives propels us to do whatever it takes to pursue a life of holiness and be people of personal integrity.

Really, in the end, it is our conviction that God has a call for our lives and we have a personal responsibility to do all that we can to complete that call that motivates us to do whatever it takes to be able to say as Paul did at the end of his life:

> *As for me, my life has already been poured out as an offering to God.*
>
> *The time of my death is near.*
>
> *I have fought the good fight, I have finished the race, and I have remained faithful.*
>
> *And now the prize awaits me—the crown of righteousness, which the Lord, the righteous Judge, will give me on the day of his return.*
>
> *And the prize is not just for me but for all who eagerly look forward to his appearing. (2 Timothy 4:6-8, NLT)*

Essentially, Paul was saying, *"At the end of my life, I can say with a clear conscience when I stand before God that I did whatever it took to fulfill the call He placed on my life."*

The radical challenge all of us have to answer is: At the end of our lives, when we are called to give an account to God, will we be able to say the same thing?

Will we, with a good conscience, be able to say, *"I did whatever it took. I gave it all I had. I left everything on the field. I sincerely did the best I could"*?

Ultimately, this should be the goal of every follower of God.

Just as we all have a calling, each one has a personal responsibility to make this our lifelong motto: *"Whatever it takes, I'll do it for God."*

Perhaps you're thinking, *"It's too late for me to be able to say that. I've already blown it and spent too many years of my life pursuing anything but the will of God."*

Maybe your story isn't a life filled with sin, but instead, you've led a life of apathy, choosing rather to be a casual Christian whose life is filled with compromise rather than doing whatever it takes to follow God and fulfill His call on your life.

Here's an amazing truth: You can still have Paul's testimony.

After all, remember that Paul spent the early part of his life as a spiritual bounty hunter persecuting Christians. In those days, his passion wasn't advancing the Gospel, but rather doing whatever it took to destroy Christianity. This included persecuting and killing Christians.

Paul describes himself this way in 1 Timothy 1:15-16:

> *This is a trustworthy saying, and everyone should accept it: "Christ Jesus came into the world to save sinners"—and I*

> *am the worst of them all.*
>
> *But God had mercy on me so that Christ Jesus could use me as a prime example of his great patience with even the worst sinners.*
>
> *Then others will realize that they, too, can believe in him and receive eternal life. (NLT)*

I love these verses because Paul is basically saying, *"Look at me! I was the worst of sinners—-a prime example that anyone can change through the power of God."*

Today, his testimony can be your testimony. No matter what happened in your past or what choices you've made until now, you can make a different choice.

Like Paul, you can decide that you are done wasting your life in the chains of sin. You're done living your life for yourself and your pleasure. Instead, you can make the choice to do whatever it takes to live your life wholeheartedly for God and fulfill the call He has for your life.

You can start by asking God to forgive you for the days you've spent not doing whatever it takes, and then complete the repentance cycle by determining from this day forward that you will do whatever it takes—seriously whatever—to live for God, to obey His commands, to pursue your calling, and to live a life worthy of the calling that you have received.

It isn't over until it's over. As long as you are living you can still make the choice to follow God with all of your heart, mind, soul, and strength.

Today, God is calling you to live a life of boldness—doing whatever it takes to follow Him.

Just like Peter and Paul, God has a plan for your life.

The question now rests with you: Do you want to walk in your call?

Are you convinced that living for God is worth doing whatever He asks with all of your heart?

Will you commit today to allow this conviction to become a driving passion in every action, decision, and direction you take for the remainder of your days?

Do you want to be able to say at the end of your life, *"I did whatever it took to follow God?"*

The opportunity is here. What will you choose?

Group Study Questions:

1. What keeps you going when you want to quit?

2. When was the last time someone questioned your convictions?

3. How does conviction keep us from sinning?

4. At the end of your life, when you are called to give an account of yourself to God, can you say with a clear conscience that you did whatever it took to fulfill your calling? What do you need to change to make this statement true?

5. Will you commit today to allow this conviction to become a driving passion in every action, decision, and direction you take for the remainder of your days?

6. After reading this chapter, what is one thing you will put into practice or one thing you will change in your life?

7. How can we as a group help you do this?

Radical Challenge:

It's time to answer the most important questions of all:

Do you want to be able to say at the end of your life, *"I did whatever it took to follow God's will for my life?"*

What needs to change in your life so Paul's epitaph will be your epitaph?

I challenge you to spend some time with these questions and write down your answers. Then do whatever it takes to fulfill your God-given calling. Remember: Defeat is not an option.

WHATEVER IT TAKES

Workbook

Workbook

Chapter One:

-"Whatever it takes, yes, Lord Jesus, I will _____ _____ in every area of my life."

-Choosing to follow Jesus and walk in your calling will require work and _____, obedience and _____.
However, it will also reap rewards that are beyond anything you can imagine.

Do you want to walk in God's call for your life?

Write down what you feel your call is:

What can you do to take that first step to walk in this call?

Radical Challenge:

We must all remember our memorial stones—the moments when we hear God's call either to salvation or when He reveals a portion of His will for our lives.

Whatever It Takes

This chapter's radical challenge is to take some time and remember one of these experiences. Record the incident on paper or a computer. Place it somewhere that you will always remember your commitment to do whatever it takes to follow God's will for your life.

Group Study Questions:

1. How is accepting God's call similar to a marriage engagement?

2. What has been hindering you from walking confidently into God's calling?

3. This chapter stated, *"Choosing to follow God and walk in your calling will require work and sacrifice, obedience and calling."* What does this mean to you?

4. As you discover your calling, are you willing to do whatever it takes to walk in your calling?

5. After reading this chapter, what is one thing you will put into practice or one thing you will change in your life?

6. How can we as a group help you do this?

Chapter 2:

-God's plan for your life doesn't just involve _____, but instead, it involves the lives of _____ _____ that He wants you to reach and influence for the kingdom of God.

-We need to be aware that our lives are not just our _____—we belong to _____.

-Who can you influence for the Kingdom of God?

Radical Challenge:

Do you realize that YOU were not born to simply earn enough money to survive, live out your days in monotony, or experience as much pleasure as possible?

Do you recognize that God has a unique purpose just for you—that purpose includes influencing people in your sphere of influence for the kingdom of God?

As a practical step, grab a sheet of paper and make a list of the people in your life—including family, friends, co-workers, people in your community. Ask God, *"How do You want me to influence them for You?"*

Group Study Questions:

1. What do you believe is your calling in life?

2. What does *"With great privilege comes great responsibility"* mean to you?

3. How does submitting to your God-given calling resemble joining the armed services?

4. How does this analogy change the way you think about your calling?

5. How does it affect other people when you do not walk in your calling?

6. Are you willing to embrace God's calling?

7. After reading this chapter, what is one thing you will put into practice or one thing you will change in your life?

8. How can we as a group help you do this?

Chapter Three

-"Calling" puts the responsibility on _____ to decide who is "allowed" to do what in His _____.

-The phrase "_____ *calling"* is very important. God doesn't call us all to do the _____ _____.

Write in your own words why you don't have choices when it comes to calling:

Radical Challenge:

Make a list of the decisions you currently need to make in your life.

Commit to seeking God's will in prayer about each decision. As the Holy Spirit leads you in each area, take a moment and write down how God directed you in each choice. Then follow God's leading even if it is different than you originally planned.

Commit to making this a new practice in your life.

Group Study Questions:

1. Why do you think we struggle with looking at other people's calling instead of focusing on what God has called us to do?

2. Why is it unbiblical to say that we, as God's children, can have any life we choose and have everything we want?

3. How do we discover our unique calling?

4. What practical steps can you take to encourage others to follow their unique calling?

5. Are you passionately pursuing your calling?

6. After reading this chapter, what is one thing you will put into practice or one thing you will change in your life?

7. How can we as a group help you do this?

Chapter 4:

-As followers of God seeking to live a life worthy of our calling, we are to be as _____ with the _____ of _____ as a sheep is to its shepherd's voice.

-Until we recognize the importance of something we don't really _____ it.

How do we hear God's voice?

When do you spend time with God? Write it down.

Where do spend time with God? Write it down.

Write down your plan to read the Bible:

Radical Challenge:

Sit down and create a plan to spend time with God.

Decide:

When is the best time for you to read the Bible and pray?

Where is the best place?

Who do you need to share your plan with so you won't be interrupted?

Are there other distractions (like your phone or computer) that you need to remove from your prayer time?

What Bible reading plan will you do?

Once you've created a plan—start doing it every day. If you need accountability, who will help you stick to your commitment?

Group Study Questions:

1. What does it mean to be "familiar" with the voice of God?

2. How do we develop this familiarity?

3. Do you have a set time to get alone with God to hear his voice?

4. What is one thing you can sacrifice to spend time alone with God?

5. Where do you spend time with God? How do you avoid distractions?

6. After reading this chapter, what is one thing you will put into practice or one thing you will change in your life?

7. How can we as a group help you do this?

Chapter 5

-Jesus told the disciples that the Holy Spirit would _____ them all things and _____ them of everything Jesus said to them.

-The Baptism in the Holy Spirit is how *we* go from just ordinary people to people who can _____ and _____ the world around us for the kingdom of God.

If you have been baptized in the Holy Spirit, write down your experience/testimony:

Radical Challenge:

This chapter said: "*It is the responsibility of every believer to seek the baptism of the Holy Spirit. After we have received it, we are responsible to be active in our prayer language on a consistent basis.*"

Are you accepting your responsibility?

If you are not baptized in the Holy Spirit, commit to seeking this gift today.

If you have been baptized in the Holy Spirit, commit to using your prayer language each day.

Group Study Questions:

1. This chapter talked about how the baptism in the Holy Spirit changed the lives of the disciples—share what their stories mean to you.

2. Why is it important to be filled with the Spirit to fulfill the Great Commission?

3. Have you been baptized in the Holy Spirit? Share your testimony.

4. Why do you think some people are filled immediately while others take more time?

5. Do you regularly use your prayer language?

6. After reading this chapter, what is one thing you will put into practice or one thing you will change in your life?

7. How can we as a group help you do this?

Chapter 6

-The challenge in this chapter that stands before each of us is *"Are we willing to be _____ of _____?"*

-Faith means that because you believe God has told you to do something you do it with with all of the _____, _____, _____, and _____ that you have.

-Living by faith doesn't remove our obligation to _____. Instead, our faith should compel us to _____ _____ because we believe that we are working for God.

What step of faith is God asking you to take to walk in your calling? Write it down:

Radical Challenge:

This chapter says: *"When deciding whether or not to take a step of faith we need to ask ourselves, 'Do I want to please God?'"*

What step of faith is God asking you to take to walk in your calling?

How can you walk in obedience?

Recognize the first step you need to take and then take it.

Group Study Questions:

1. Why does God often require us to take leaps of faith when we walk in our calling?

2. Have you ever refused to take a leap of faith that God was asking you to do? What caused you to resist taking the leap?

3. What was the last leap of faith God called you to take?

4. What does the phrase *"Pray as though everything depended on God; act as though everything depended on you"* mean?

5. Do you want to live a life of faith or fear? How do you make your answer happen?

6. After reading this chapter, what is one thing you will put into practice or one thing you will change in your life?

7. How can we as a group help you do this?

Chapter 7

-Seeing a vision become a reality requires a lot of
_____. Whether or not you are willing to endure and embrace this truth, often determines whether or not you will see God's vision for your life _____.

How can you invest in learning? Write down a plan of action:

What specifically do you need to sacrifice to walk in your calling? Write it down and the steps you will take to do it:

Radical Challenge:

Take a moment and ask yourself: *"What call has God placed on my heart? What is my dream? What do I believe God is asking me to do to advance His kingdom?"*

Write your answers down.

Now answer a more difficult question:

"What investments are necessary for me to fulfill my God-given call?"

"What sacrifices do I need to make?"

Again, write down these answers.

Next, write down three practical steps you can take to start making this investment.

1.

2.

3.

Then, next to each practical step, challenge yourself by writing down a deadline for when to start taking the practical step.

Finally, do whatever it takes to start investing in following God's call on your life.

Group Study Questions:

1. What is the cost of walking in your calling?

2. What will walking in your calling require you to sacrifice?

3. What class can you take or book can you read to gain more knowledge to walk in your calling?

4. This chapter stated: "*You can't walk in the anointing of the Holy Spirit if you aren't spending time with Him.*" What does this mean in your life?

5. How can you overcome the *"somedays"* that attack you? What have you been putting off that you need to do?

6. Is God's call worth the investment?

7. After reading this chapter, what is one thing you will put into practice or one thing you will change in your life?

8. How can we as a group help you do this?

Chapter 8

-Pride makes us blindly unaware to all of the things that we don't _____. It hides our _____, our lack of _____, and our deep need to _____ from others.

-Humility is the ability to admit that you don't _____ what you don't _____.

How has pride kept you from walking in your calling? Write down examples:

Who is someone who has been a mentor to you? Write down the biggest influence they have had on your life:

Radical Challenge:

Is God trying to bring a mentor into your life?

Analyze yourself and ask, *"How can I gain the most from this relationship?"*

Look at the tips above and determine what attitudes in your heart need to change and what new attitudes need to be developed so that you can learn as much as you can from your mentor.

Make a list and then start making the changes.

Group Study Questions:

1. Why is humility so important to walking in our calling?

2. Do you have a mentor? How have they influenced your life?

3. Has God been trying to bring a mentor into your life, but you've been resisting? Really look at your life and see if you are missing a blessing.

4. Why should you be respectful of their time?

5. Why is it important to do what your mentor tells you to do?

6. This chapter talked about "*not expecting a participation trophy from your mentor*". It's a funny way to put it, but how should you properly respond to criticism?

7. After reading this chapter, what is one thing you will put into practice or one thing you will change in your life?

8. How can we as a group help you do this?

Chapter 9

-Even though _____ _____ and even sometimes popular _____ _____ about what may be right or wrong may change over the years, God's word does not.

-It's time we abandon both _____ as well as _____ and live the way the _____ tells us to live.

How is alcohol a cheap replacement for the Holy Spirit?

Write down three things you need to change in your life to pursue holiness so you can walk in your calling:

1.

2.

3.

Radical Challenge:

Spend some time with the Holy Spirit answering these questions:

"Are there any areas of my life where I need to do a better job of pursuing purity and godliness?"

"Am I compromising and making excuses rather than obeying God's Word?"

Dare to be hard on yourself. Ask:

"Why am I embracing the culture instead of God's ways?"

"Who is influencing my choices and are they a good influence?"

"Is the excuse, 'Well, everybody else is doing it' really a valid argument?"

"Are there areas where I need to reevaluate and perhaps abandon my choices?"

"If I stay on my current path, what sin will I be tolerating 15 years from now?"

Finally, make the lifestyle changes necessary to do whatever it takes to pursue godliness and live a life worthy of your calling.

Group Study Questions:

1. Why is godly living so important for a believer?

2. This chapter stated, *"It's time we abandon both legalism as well as compromising and just live the way the Bible tells us to live."* What does this mean?

3. What are some of the influences in your life that need to be abandoned if you want to live a godly life?

4. Are there any areas of your life where you need to do a better job of pursuing purity and godliness?

5. Are you compromising and making excuses rather than obeying God's Word?

6. After reading this chapter, what is one thing you will put into practice or one thing you will change in your life?

7. How can we as a group help you do this?

Chapter 10:

-Personal _____ is an integral part of living a life worthy of your calling.

-First, don't make any _____ unless you are really committed to _____ them. Second, if you've made a commitment, do everything in your power to _____ your _____.

What steps do you take/need to take to have integrity in relationships with the opposite sex? Write it/them down:

What area of integrity did the Holy Spirit convict you of in this chapter? Write it down and what you will do to change:

Radical Challenge:

Take some time and evaluate yourself in all four of these areas.

Ask yourself: In which area do I struggle most? Where do I need to improve?

Take it a step further and ask the most honest person in your life if they see any areas in your life that lack integrity.

Now look at your weakest area and write down three practical steps that you can take to begin walking in personal integrity. Then start doing whatever it takes to change your reputation.

1.

2.

3.

Group Study Questions:

1. How does integrity work with walking in your calling?

2. How do you demonstrate integrity in your finances? What steps can you take to have even more financial integrity?

3. Why is it important to always keep your commitments?

4. Why is it important to be a person of integrity as you interact with the opposite sex?

5. What practical steps do you need to implement in your interactions?

6. In what area of your life do you struggle the most to be a person of integrity?

7. What practical steps can you take to improve?

8. After reading this chapter, what is one thing you will put into practice or one thing you will change in your life?

9. How can we as a group help you do this?

Chapter 11:

- That's what it means to truly take on the challenge to do whatever it takes to follow God—to love Him with of all of your _____, all of your _____, and all of your _____.

- We show love to people by doing what Jesus said and _____ people the way that you would want to be _____.

- Like a light in the darkness, treating people with _____ and showing them _____ helps people identify Christians as _____.

Write down what convicted you most in this chapter and what three steps you can take to change:

1.

2.

3.

What action can you make a habit to exhibit love to others? Write it down, be specific:

Radical Challenge:

Take a moment and list the people in your sphere of influence. Start with the inner circle of your immediate family and move out including the people who live near you, who work near you, the people you carpool with to work or school, your friends and your enemies, the other parents at your children's school or on their sports team, the woman at the grocery store, the guy at the restaurant.

Ask the Holy Spirit to show you three practical ways that you can demonstrate love to the people in your life in the next week. What habits, attitudes, or actions would He like you to change?

1.

2.

3.

Finally, determine to begin making these practical changes and doing whatever it takes to fulfill your calling by walking in love.

Group Study Questions:

1. How does walking in our calling require a genuine love of God?

2. What are the specific actions you can start taking to show love to those around you?

3. Are you willing to show love by meeting the needs of others no matter what it costs you personally?

4. Are you listening to the voice of the Holy Spirit when He shows you a practical need that you can meet? Are you responding in obedience? How can you do better?

5. What can you do to better demonstrate the love of Jesus in your life?

6. After reading this chapter, what is one thing you will put into practice or one thing you will change in your life?

7. How can we as a group help you do this?

Chapter 12:

-Conviction is the deep, unshakeable believe that convinces you that what you are doing is _____ _____ for your life combined with the deep _____ belief that the center of God's will is the only place you want to be.

-The conviction that following God is worth doing whatever it takes is what keeps us on the _____ and _____ choosing not to engage in _____ even for a moment.

What are three convictions you hold deeply:

1.

2.

3.

Eventually, your convictions will be challenged. Write down how you will respond to these challenges so you are prepared ahead of time:

Radical Challenge:

It's time to answer the most important questions of all:

Do you want to be able to say at the end of your life, ***"I did whatever it took to follow God's will for my life?"***

What needs to change in your life so Paul's epitaph will be your epitaph?

I challenge you to spend some time with these questions and write down your answers. Then do whatever it takes to fulfill your God-given calling. Remember: Defeat is not an option.

Group Study Questions:

1. What keeps you going when you want to quit?

2. When was the last time someone questioned your convictions?

3. How does conviction keep us from sinning?

4. At the end of your life, when you are called to give an account of yourself to God, can you say with a clear conscience that you did whatever it took to fulfill your calling? What do you need to change to make this statement true?

5. Will you commit today to allow this conviction to become a driving passion in every action, decision, and direction you take for the remainder of your days?

6. After reading this chapter, what is one thing you will put into practice or one thing you will change in your life?

7. How can we as a group help you do this?

Fill In Answers

Chapter 1
- follow you
- sacrifice, commitment

Chapter 2
- you, every person
- own, God

Chapter 3
- God, kingdom
- unique, same thing

Chapter 4
- familiar, voice, God
- prioritize

Chapter 5
- teach, remind
- change, influence

Chapter 6
- people, faith
- effort, passion, energy, strength
- work, work harder,

Chapter 7
- sacrifice, fulfilled

Chapter 8
- know, weaknesses, experience, learn
- know, know

Chapter 9
- society's standard, church opinion
- legalism, compromising, Bible

Chapter 10
- integrity
- commitments, keeping, honor, word

Chapter 11
- passion, intelligence, energy
- treat, treated
- respect, love, different

Chapter 12
- God's Will, unshakeable
- straight, narrow, sin

Bibliography

Chapter 1

1. Chapman, Steven Curtis, "For the Sake of the Call" For the Sake of the Call, Sparrow Records, 1990, Track #1.

Chapter 2

1. *Spider-Man*. (2002). [film] Directed by S. Raimi. USA: Columbia Pictures Corporation & Marvel Enterprises.

Chapter 4

1. Barker, Kennth L. And John R. Kohlenberger III. *Zondervan NIV Bible Commentary Vol 2: New Testament.* Grand Rapids, MI: Zondervan Publishing House, 1994.

Chapter 5

1. Edersheim, Alfred. *The Life and Times of Jesus the Messiah.* Peabody, MA: Hendrickson Publishers, Inc., 1993.

2. Enloe, Tim. *Want More? Experience Greater Spiritual Intimacy and Power Through the Holy Spirit Baptism.* E.M. Publications; Third Edition, 2004.

Chapter 7

1. Lindsey Elizabeth, "Megachurch Pastor Issues Urgent Warning to Christians Who Do Yoga". *Faithwire 2018,* https://www.faithwire.com/2018/11/27/megachurch-pastor-warns-of-yogas-demonic-roots

2. Assemblies of God Positions Paper "Abstinence from Alcohol (ADOPTED BY THE GENERAL PRESBYTERY IN SESSION AUGUST 2-3, 2016)"; website: https://ag.org/Beliefs/Position-Papers/Abstinence-from-Alcohol. Downloaded June 25, 2019.

3. Above the Influence. https://abovetheinfluence.com/

3. Eric Munson, CPP, ICPS. "DRUGS & ALCOHOL 101". *Heidi's Promise: Choices Today Affect Tomorrow. 2010,* http://heidispromise.org/Resources/Drugs-Alcohol-101/Alcohol-Facts

ALSO AVAILABLE FROM MANTOUR MINISTRIES

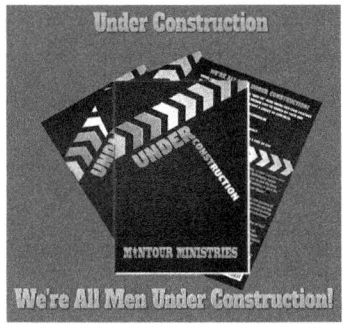

**Available in print and digital formats.
Visit www.mantourministries.com
for more information.**

    Jamie loves to speak to men and is available to speak at your next men's event. Jamie combines humor and his personal testimony to both engage and challenge men to grow in their walk with God. He uses his testimony of overcoming abuse as well as dealing with his physical and emotional issues growing up to encourage men that no matter what their background or where they have come from in life, they can grow into mighty men in God's kingdom.

    "Years ago, while I was attending the University of Valley Forge, God gave me a deep desire to minister to men. My calling is to help men learn what it means to be a godly man and how to develop a deep, personal relationship with their heavenly Father. We strive to challenge and encourage men to reach their full potential in God's kingdom."

    If you are interested in having Jamie at your next men's event as a speaker or workshop leader, or if you are interested in having him come share with your church, e-mail him at jamie@mantourministries.com. He is also available to speak for one or multiple weeks on the theme of his books, Whatever It Takes, Invincible: Scaling The Mountains That Keep Us From Victory. Putting On Manhood, Legacy: Living a Life that Lasts, and Get in the Game.

PURCHASE A BOOK FOR A PRISONER

If you enjoyed this book, why not buy a copy for a man in prison. You can help us reach more men behind bars by donating at mantourministries.com.

Mantour Ministries donates copies of our curriculum to state and federal prisons. We are reaching men behind bars with the gospel!

Partner with the Ministry:

JAMIE HOLDEN

FOUNDER/DIRECTOR, MANTOUR MINISTRIES

SCAN WITH PHONE CAMERA

GIVE ONLINE AT
HTTPS://WWW.MANTOURMINISTRIES.COM/PARTNER

www.ingramcontent.com/pod-product-compliance
Lightning Source LLC
LaVergne TN
LVHW051520070426
835507LV00023B/3205